Menopause

MENOPAUSE

The Inner Journey

Susanne F. Fincher

SHAMBHALA

Boston & London
1995

Shambhala Publications, Inc.
Horticultural Hall
300 Massachusetts Avenue
Boston, Massachusetts 02115

The quotation on page v is from Rainer Maria Rilke, *Duino Elegies,*
trans. David Young (New York: W. W. Norton & Co., 1992).
Reprinted by permission of the publisher.

9   8   7   6   5   4   3   2   1

First Edition
Printed in the United States of America on acid-free paper ♾
Distributed in the United States by Random House, Inc.,
and in Canada by Random House of Canada Ltd

Library of Congress Cataloging-in-Publication Data

Fincher, Susanne F., 1941–
    Menopause: the inner journey / Susanne F. Fincher. — 1st ed.
      p.   cm.
    Includes bibliographical references.
    ISBN 1-57062-152-7 (alk. paper)
    1. Life change events—Religious aspects.   2. Spiritual life—New
Age movement.   3. Fincher, Susanne F., 1941–   .   4. Menopause—
Psychological aspects.   5. Middle aged women—Religious life.
6. Aged women—Religious life.   7. New Age movement.   I. Title.
BP605.N48F54   1995   95-8697
291.4′4′0844—dc20   CIP

Then the whole cycle of change finds its first origin
in the seasons of our life.

—Rainer Maria Rilke,
Fourth Elegy
(Trans. David Young)

Contents

Acknowledgments

Thanks to Henry, who was the first to teach me about rituals and personal growth; to Maurus, who was present at crucial turning points during my growing; to Lila, who taught me about the healing power of art; and to Jesse, who accompanied me on my journey. They are all part of this book, one way or another.

Thanks also to my sister Marilyn for reading chapters and making helpful suggestions at every stage in the development of this work; and to my parents, Art and Ada Wre, for their support, understanding, and encouragement.

Menopause

Introduction

The passage from middle-aged to elder, marked for women by the menopause, happens around the fiftieth year. From my own experience and that of friends and acquaintances, I know that menopause is a major turning point in one's life. It may be experienced as an initiation into a new status, that of the "youth of old age." I prefer to call it becoming a crone. Our culture does not support this transition with rituals, and it is made particularly difficult by our worship of youth and the resulting devaluation of the status of elder. We are advised to think of menopause as a disease rather than a gateway to a new way of life. It is this passage into cronedom about which this book is written. While the book focuses on the personal transformation accompanying menopause, the patterns identified in the process of transition are applicable to other times of change as well.

This book was birthed out of the turmoil marking my transition from middle-aged woman to young crone. My journey began with the command to "make ritual," given to me in a dream. It was a painful passage that ultimately set me free in some ways I never could have foreseen. My journey demanded nothing less than the surrender of who I thought I was. Panic, depression, anger, and loss of hope marked my descent. Trusting, waiting, and weeping over the broken pieces accompanied my deepest passage. Then delight, love, and renewed hope came as my very identity was transformed. Finally, the full discovery and acceptance of once-disowned talents, abilities, and knowledge gave me an expanded sense of self more powerful and resilient than before. As with all good initiations, I have arrived on the other side with a deepened sense of who I am and a stronger connection to that mysterious Other with whom I share my psychic space.

As I marked my transition to another stage of life, I became aware that my pathway was not a linear one. It was a spiraling path that dropped deep into the mystery of inner reality, where things were softened, taken apart, and dissolved. Then slowly it climbed upward, bringing together the pieces of myself into a new pattern, a strengthened ego structure.

Tales from the mythologies of Greece, Egypt, and Mesopotamia comforted me on my journey. Like Persephone, I felt that I had been snatched from a pleasant, sunny place and plunged into a dark, sad underworld against my will. Like the goddess Inanna, I was compelled to move deeper and deeper into the darkness, reluctantly surrendering treasured artifacts of identity as I went, until at last I too felt dead, rotten, and abandoned. Like Isis, I had the task of finding all the bloody pieces and putting them back together. And like Ariadne, I met the challenge of finding my way back to the light with love, creativity, and relationship.

The stories of the myths offered a map of the way in and out of the darkness. They showed me that I must not turn back and gave me courage to press on with the journey. I learned that the journey is above all a time of solitude, and yet there are others along the way who can help. I found that giving myself up to the experience of the moment, whether painful or full of joy, stretched my sense of who I was and made me less afraid of what life has to offer.

Rituals, informal rituals connected with my inner work, became important to me during the long months of transition. They provided a container for the intense feelings I experienced. Rituals allowed me to do something concrete at moments when I felt helpless. They made sense of the events I was remembering, reliving, and trying to make peace with. Rituals gave voice to my awe of the power that moves behind a human life and sends us healing whether we want it or not.

1

The Call

"Make ritual," the voice said. As I woke up, I looked around the room to see who had spoken. My husband was sleeping quietly next to me. We were alone. "Make ritual," I repeated to myself thickly. The directive had brought me from a deep sleep into consciousness, but I was still a little fuzzy. Obviously, it was an inner voice that had spoken.

I had heard these words before. But when? Where? Then my mind lit up with a colorful memory. It was at the end of a week-long conference. Lance, an eloquent spokesman for the earth-centered religion of his mother, a Cherokee, led us in a closing ritual. As we handed a sacred tobacco pipe around the circle, he spoke of the relatedness of all beings, of the sense of communion created by the sharing of the ritual act of smoking, and of the smoke as a carrier of our prayers for peace back into the world. He talked of the importance of ceremony for all peoples as a way to connect themselves with the deeper reality that gives life vitality. He urged each of us, in our own way, to "make ritual."

I had identified the source of the memory, but why had it come to me now? Little did I know that I had set my foot upon a path that would transform me and my comfortable ideas about who I knew myself to be. Like Persephone, I was about to be plunged into darkness. In preparation for my journey inward, the unconscious gave me the key to survival. Ritual was to sustain me, bring me healing, and mark my transition from woman to crone.

My fiftieth birthday came at a time when I was riding high. My first book had been published a few months earlier. Things were going well for my family as our two oldest children navigated their transition to young-adult independence. I gave little thought to the changes that would be coming my way because of growing older. I certainly felt like a kid inside. The forties had dragged on, a tedious end to youth, but turning fifty shifted me into a new ballgame: the second half of life. I felt like a novice. I began to look for older women who were living active lives to see just what the parameters of this new game were.

One of the best examples of aging I saw was my friend Sister Maurus, an indefatigable Roman Catholic nun who led retreats for women, taught yoga, and traveled frequently to eastern Europe, Russia, and the Middle East from her Southern monastery. Maurus and I often worked together at conferences, and soon after my fiftieth birthday we were roommates at a retreat center in North Carolina. Maurus knew about my birthday, and she came prepared to perform a croning ceremony. One night in our room she presented me with a beautiful necklace as a symbol of my new status as a crone. We toasted the occasion with paper cups of bourbon and 7-Up. I felt deeply honored to be welcomed into the sisterhood of cronedom, but I did not really have a sense of myself as an elder.

I got little help from the ordinary ideas about older women. Our culture loves the maiden and accepts the woman, but views the old woman with ambivalence. She is most often

portrayed as either a kindly, asexual grandmother or a dangerous, twisted old witch. I wanted something in between for
myself. Looking at the lives of women in other cultures, I
discovered that women often assume positions of leadership
and authority once their childbearing years are behind them.
Margaret Mead (1928) wrote of the elevated status of post-
menopausal women in South Pacific cultures. As elders they
stepped out of the close-knit circle of family and into involve-
ment in the larger community, there to share the wisdom they
had earned from years of birthing and rearing their children.
Native Americans had a similarly positive attitude about older
women. They said that with menopause a woman was saving
her blood for growing wisdom.

Looking toward the more positive aspects of becoming a
crone, I opened myself to the transition marked by menopause. I had weathered change before, so I felt confident about
what life held for me. Little did I realize that the hormonal
changes in my body would set in motion such unexpected
turmoil. The hot flashes I began to experience made me feel
as if a fire had been lit down below. Some sort of psychic
cooking process had indeed begun, a procedure that was to
render the fat from bones. The fat was those cultural values
about what a woman should look like, how she should behave,
and what the prescribed limits of aging were. That garbage was
to be melted away, leaving behind a tough, lean, tender, joyful
crone.

I developed an affinity for bones. I collected the skeletons
of birds and sea creatures, and stones, the bones of the earth,
and placed them on a table in my bedroom along with other
precious things. Wearing black just felt right. I listened with
deep intensity to what other women had to say about their
experiences, and I paid attention to the messages from my unconscious in dreams and body symptoms.

The cooking process in those deeply hidden areas where psyche and soma blend together began sending to the surface pieces of information that had not been conscious for years. I took my task to be chewing, digesting, and drawing nourishment from the memories that came up. This was an incredible challenge because some of the information called into question my core beliefs about who I was.

The unconscious guards your childhood memories. By discovering what has been lost, forgotten, or repressed from the past, you enrich who you are, connecting the different parts of yourself into an ever more unified pattern. In order to do this work you must be willing to revise who you think you are. You must be willing to incorporate surprising truths about yourself. Though difficult, the work is worthwhile because you grow in wisdom and integrity through this process. Sometimes it seems that a growth spurt is dictated by benevolent forces within the psyche itself that steer you into new territory. I became aware that I was being taken for such a ride when I had a vivid dream.

I was riding on a bus. It was a very long bus with joints so it could bend. I was sitting in the back. Defying the rules of safe driving, the bus driver speeded up instead of slowing down around corners. The centrifugal force whipped the end of the bus around incredibly fast, and I hung on as best I could. The bus was like a huge snake, bending and whipping. I could not believe the driver was doing this, but he seemed to know what he was doing and somehow things were working all right.

Then the bus careened around another corner. My body was pressed hard against the side of the passenger compartment and my face was flattened against the window. The bus crashed over the sidewalk and smashed against the front of buildings there. Pedestrians scrambled to get out of the way, but some fell down and the bus rolled over them. I was horrified by what appeared to be a terrible accident. I threw myself around to look back and saw that, miraculously, no one was hurt. The driver thought nothing of all this chaos he was creating, and continued his breakneck speed.

The sinuous form of the bus suggested something lifelike. To me it recalled the Indian symbol for life force, or kundalini, that is conceptualized as a snake coiled at the base of the spinal column, present in potential at the moment of conception. This metaphorical snake is the source of etheric energy that flows upward through the spinal column. At certain nodal points, known as chakras in the Hindu tradition, the energy is transformed as it surges from the base of the spine to the top of the head. The process of kundalini rising is a helpful image for understanding the interplay between natural biological processes and the conscious intention to bring meaning to experience.

In my dream I was being taken for a ride in a vehicle with a driver who knew where he was going. He represented the ease and sureness of a natural process operating smoothly as it had for thousands of years. While all was calm and organized at his end of the bus, things appeared dangerous and chaotic at my end. Without awareness of the process represented by the driver and the bus, all I saw was disorder. It was a scary ride, but no one was injured. My unconscious was showing me that the energy of life was moving me around, and that although it was frightening, all was going just as it should be.

The unconscious relentlessly offers you what you need to know in order to balance your psyche. These communications, when heeded, guide you toward becoming who you are truly meant to be. If at first you do not correctly interpret the message, it comes in another form. The messages from the unconscious become more and more adamant when repeatedly ignored or misinterpreted.

Information that is truly helpful to you may sometimes even be presented as nightmares if you disregard the wisdom in your ordinary dreams. For weeks the unconscious had been offering me wisdom that I had not understood. Finally the message came in a form I could not deny: the powerful voice that had jolted me awake with the command, "Make ritual!"

OK, fine. I got it. But *what* ritual? And what for?

Perhaps the unconscious was directing me to write a book about rituals, I reasoned. In hopes that my activity would satisfy the muse, I plunged into research about rituals. The work went well. I enjoyed my summer vacation devouring books by the swimming pool. The voice was silent, which I took as affirmation, and by the end of summer I had a rough draft of my first chapter.

The Cramp

Meanwhile, subtle changes had been taking place in my body. In August, shortly before my fifty-first birthday, I missed a period. My body was in a state of high tension. Always before, this premenstrual tension was dissolved when my period began, but this time, without the release of a period, it was as if my body continued to tighten to the point of a total body cramp. The cramping began to coalesce around a spot near my heart. It seemed as if I had a lump lodged right under my breastbone.

Then, to my surprise, I found that the food I ate would not pass into my stomach. That lump was a cramp in my esophagus. Liquids trickled through, but there was the possibility that the cramping would increase and I would be forced to rely on feeding tubes for nourishment. This possibility terrified me. I envisioned myself starving to death because of an innocuous muscle cramp for which I felt somehow responsible but over which I seemingly had no control.

My body, whose dependable functioning I largely took for granted, had suddenly demanded my full attention. I felt angry, frustrated, and bewildered, as if an old friend had turned against me with no warning. I arranged for the recommended medical tests, but during the week it took to perform the tests and get the results, I pondered the meaning of all this. Considering that body symptoms also communicate information from the unconscious (Mindell 1982), I decided to spend the week doing intensive inner work, meditation, and ceremony in an effort to bring to consciousness what it was that I "could not swallow."

My body had dictated a minor health crisis, but I still had the option to view it as I chose. I could see it as merely a health problem and shift all responsibility for my healing to others, or I could see the cramp as a metaphor for something else, some teaching I was to receive. Because I took some responsibility for my body's symptoms, I felt a need to participate consciously in the healing through activities that honored the mysterious process of which I felt myself a part.

It seemed that the unconscious, through body symptoms, was imposing a food fast. Fasting is used for ritual purification in cultures all over the world. Perhaps my body was telling me to prepare for something important, possibly some sort of initiation. I cleared my calendar and prepared to make ritual.

The inner work of creating and performing a ritual might possibly release information into consciousness that would relieve my body symptoms. I hoped the ritual work would open the connection between body and soul and help me regain my emotional equilibrium. Being careful not to neglect my physical needs, I purchased a week's supply of liquid-diet food, which I could still get down.

The morning of my decision to begin ritual work I felt a ripple of excitement about what might be coming. I sat quietly in meditation and counted my breaths. I imagined my body bathed in soft, soothing colors. My shoulders relaxed, but my restless hands would not be still.

To keep my hands busy while meditating, I began work on a ceremonial hat for myself. I had had the materials on hand for at least a year but had not made time to work on it because I felt it was arrogant of me to want such a hat. That attitude no longer mattered, and I set to work wrapping feathers, stringing beads, and sewing on tiny images of animals. As I worked with the symbolic objects, I thought about my life and the possibility of dying.

Life and death seemed so contradictory that I felt they could not possibly coexist. One is either alive or dead. Then I thought about unfortunates who are dead in a meaningless life. I remembered the dead who live on in their music and art. And I remembered my grandmothers, who live on in me in the patterns of body and mind I have inherited from them.

My thoughts turned to my own daughters and granddaughters and of how I, too, would live on in them past all remembrance of me as an individual. These musings comforted me and closed the contradiction between "living" and "dead." I began to see death as a dark, rich, eternal background to life, like the black background of a colorful beaded hatband. Life, with its sweet, ephemeral beauty, floats like a feather on this background of timeless nonliving. Onto my beaded hatband I sewed a tiny skull as a sign of my growing acceptance of death as a constant companion rather than a fearsome demon.

When the hat was finished, I felt strong enough to receive

more information. I addressed the blockage in my esophagus directly. "Who are you? What do you want?"

"I am a cramp," came the reply. "I am here to slow you down, to disrupt your life, to mess things up. I am just being who I am."

"You make me feel scared," I replied. "What if I can't eat? I might die. I will have to go into the hospital, not a good place to be. Can you teach me in some other way?"

"I have tried, but you won't listen. Make ritual. Make ritual. Make ritual. Don't write about it. Do it."

"I am making ritual!" I replied irritably. "I meditate. I visualize. I paint. I just made a ceremonial shaman's hat. I even visited sacred Indian mounds last week. And I am recording my dreams."

"You are supposed to do something else," the Cramp replied.

"Give me a clue," I begged.

"The twins are a clue. The twins in your dreams. Pay attention. They are your teachers," the Cramp replied enigmatically.

And so I passed the week while waiting for my doctor's call with test results. I could feel the cramp releasing little by little. The inner work had helped me relax, although it had brought an even greater mystery about what was to come. Finally my doctor called to report that the tests had shown that I did not have a serious problem. She prescribed a muscle relaxant, and the cramp was completely gone a few days later.

During the next several weeks I had four dreams of twins and young children. I dreamed I came upon two children, a boy and a girl, who were hungry, dirty, and abandoned. It was my job to care for them. A few days later I dreamed of infant twins.

I remembered Jung's contention that the doubling of an

image heralds the shift into consciousness of something that has been totally unconscious. As it crosses the threshold between conscious and unconscious, the image becomes split into two identical parts. I resolved to remain open to what the unconscious might send me.

On August 13, 1992, I wrote in my journal: "I'm feeling much better. Chest pain is gone. I'm eating solid food, a bit, with lots of liquids. Still, I feel altered, as if an important transition is at hand. I'm asking the *I Ching* to reflect the process I'm experiencing, to give me clarity about how to align myself with it."

The coin toss produced the hexagram Ken Ken (Keeping Still or Meditation), with three changing lines creating the hexagram Ken Tui (Influence or Attraction). The message of Keeping Still or Meditation was to focus on the inner perspective, attaching special importance to meditating on the object of inquiry. Furthermore, the text stated that keeping still could cause restlessness to disappear, so that one could act in harmony with the laws of the universe, thus renewing both mind and body. This seemed like an affirmation of the inner work I had undertaken to help restore my body to normal functioning.

The text for the second hexagram, Influence or Attraction, advised keeping the mind "humble and free" so as to be receptive, and further counseled staying still in the midst of influence. Regarding this hexagram Wilhelm (1977) comments that "what takes place in the depths of one's being, in the unconscious, can neither be called forth nor prevented by the conscious mind" (125). This message, like the one from the cramp, suggested that I should take an attitude of calm receptivity toward what was to come. I also felt encouraged to go more deeply into the study of rituals, letting my own experiences form the basis of my ideas.

She-Bear

As an end-of-the-summer treat for myself, I had signed up for a drum-building workshop. After the incident with the cramp, a weekend away in the cool mountains of North Carolina seemed like a nice way to shift from intensive personal work to a more lighthearted community gathering. I had been wanting a drum for a long time. Creating my own in a friendly gathering of people would make it a really special one.

The weekend was also to mark the transition from a leisurely summer schedule to a highly structured fall schedule, for I was about to begin a practicum in elementary school counseling. I was anxious about what the new schedule would be like, how it would mesh with my part-time work as an art therapist in a psychiatric hospital, and whether I would have enough personal time to nurture myself. All these fears I set aside for the weekend. I needed a rest from worry and anxiety.

Our instructor, Hawk, was a good teacher, funny, and very patient. I chose a wooden hoop and was given the elk hide for the drumhead. It was wet and soft and a little slimey. Hawk suggested we thank the animal and tree people who had donated parts of themselves for our drums. This I did quietly to myself as I cut the elk hide in a circle. I felt awkward finding the words of thanks, but saying them made me feel differently about the work. It became more than just a craft project; it was a sacred undertaking.

Building the drum was a hard day's work. First I decorated the hoop inside with a bear family, a mother and twin cubs in honor of the twins in my dreams. I punched holes in the elk hide and measured out sinew. Then came the weaving process of threading sinew through the holes, across the center of the hoop to the opposite side of the circular piece of hide, then back again. The weaving was a quiet object lesson in the necessity of returning always to the center: for making a drum and for being a person.

We held our new drums and drumsticks and listened as Hawk explained that in the Native American tradition the drum is feminine. Her shape is round, receptive like the womb. The drumstick symbolizes the masculine energy of the phallus. Apart, the drum and drumstick make no sound, but together they make the heartbeat rhythms that signal life. They belong together, like husband and wife. Together they make a whole.

We stood in a circle and sounded our drums together. The random rhythms we began with slowly settled into a patterned beat. It was a wonderful sound, there in a clearing in the woods on the side of a mountain. My body, tired moments before, began to feel energized. Refreshed by our drumming, I felt ready for whatever was next. And there was still much to be done before the end of the weekend.

The next morning we began building a small hut for a sweat lodge ceremony. Based on Native American traditions, our ritual would be a prayerful gathering in a dark saunalike atmosphere created by pouring water over heated rocks inside the hut. The intense heat of the sweat lodge causes a deep cleansing of the body through perspiration. At the same time it brings about an altered state of consciousness in which profound insights can occur. I hoped the sweat lodge would help me release any residual toxins that might have contributed to my eating problems of a few weeks earlier. It would also be an opportunity for me to search my inner knowing, and I hoped to receive some guidance for the challenges of the next few months.

It was twilight when we crawled into the dark hut. Hawk brought in red-hot rocks to place in a hole dug in the center. He closed the door flap so that we sat in complete darkness.

The water he poured over the rocks exploded instantly into steam, filling the small space with thick, scented vapor.

I felt claustrophobic as the steam heat took my breath away. The balsam boughs I was sitting on scratched my bottom. The heat was incredibly intense and burned my face and chest. My hair felt crisped, and I wondered distractedly whether I had lost it. Instinctively I pushed my hands back behind me and worked my fingertips under the blanket to feel the cool night air outside.

Hawk began the round of prayers. Each of us took a turn to say whatever he or she felt moved to say. Every once in a while Hawk splashed more water on the rocks. This brought another burst of hot steamy air into the space, but it was not such a shock as the first time. I began to relax, breathing got easier, and I got used to the sensation of sweat pouring off my body. The physical discom-

fort seemed to fall away, and it was replaced by a quiet elation.

A sweat lodge ceremony is usually divided into four rounds. Between each round the door flap is raised to allow fresh air in and to bring in more water and heated rocks. We chose to go outside the hut between rounds. Early on we drank water, made small talk, and told stories. As the rounds progressed, we grew more silent during the breaks. I felt myself going

I felt the powerful presence of She-bear during a sweat lodge ceremony.

deeper within. At the same time I began to feel a loving connection with the others in the group.

During the break after the third round Hawk invited us to meditate on animals that might have something special to say to us. As soon as the words were out of his mouth I became aware of an angry mother-bear presence, She-bear. I folded my wobbly legs and sat on the muddy ground. I began to beat the ground with my fist and make low growling noises. Then, in an instant, I *was* She-bear. As a part of me observed in awe, I growled louder, not caring what the others thought. My rage was righteous, and it gave me power. I felt indomitable, rooted in the earth, from which I drew my strength and being. My growls grew louder still and mingled with the sounds of wind, rain, and silence there on the side of the mountain.

The last round of the sweat was very peaceful. I lingered in the sweat lodge with the other women after the men had crawled out. We drummed, shared songs, talked about our experiences in the sweat. I could not say exactly what had opened for me with the connection to She-bear, but I felt that I had touched into deep recesses of myself and found there a reservoir of angry feminine power.

My compelling sweat lodge experience left me feeling as if something of great beauty had found a home deep in my belly. With calm serenity I shared in our late-evening feast and settled down for a sound night's sleep. The weekend had come to an end. In the morning I left the mountains refreshed, and I began my fall schedule the very next day.

The Memory

As part of my schoolwork I was reading about sexual abuse. I also had a personal interest in the subject. Several months earlier my brother had confided that he had memories of being sexually abused as a boy by an uncle of ours. At about the same time as his disclosure I had also heard an awful tale of abuse from a friend who works with children. I had become preoccupied with the story she told me and found myself feeling very upset about it even though the events had happened thirty years ago to people I had never known.

In an effort to free myself of the obsession, I did a painting of the image that came to mind expressing the horror of this story. It showed a naked baby lying on its back inside a flower. The baby squirmed in pain as the point of a knife sticking in its back protruded through its belly. Crouching on her hind legs and holding the flower, as if to protect and call attention to the suffering of the baby, a fierce looking she–dog bared her fangs. Her clawed feet were planted in the land of death, while around her shoulders burned flames of transformation.

I did the painting in only three days. Afterward I was shocked by its ferocity, but I felt relieved of the strong emotions that had taken me over. I hoped that through reading about sexual abuse I would come to understand what my brother was going through and perhaps gain some insight into the highly charged feelings captured in my painting.

One evening as I read a description of adult survivors of incest, I was startled to find how many of their behaviors were also mine. Searching within myself, I could find no hint of a memory of sexual abuse. Then one Sunday morning in September, a week before my fifty-first birthday, I was startled awake by what seemed to be a dream. My uncle was tucking me into bed for the night, but he was pulling my covers off and putting his hand inside my pajama bottoms. As sleep cleared, I realized this was no dream. It was a memory of being molested by the same uncle who had victimized my brother.

Now at last I understood the message of the Cramp: "The twins are a clue." My brother and I are only fourteen months apart in age. When we were small, our mother dressed us in similar outfits, and people often asked if we were twins. The twins in my dreams pointed to us.

It seemed that the gateway into cronedom was guarded by a little girl wounded by incest. To move on through, I had to embrace her and her pain. I had survived ups and downs before, but even so this initiation was to be harder than I imagined. Rituals helped me grow through to the other side.

Family Reunion

I kept to my regular schedule of activities, and things went on much as they had before. I was surprised at how much the same they were. Somehow I expected people to know, without my telling them, that I was different, and to behave differently toward me. I told my husband about my memories. His initial reaction of disbelief quickly changed to one of support, but I felt there was a strange new distance between us. It was a lonely feeling, but I needed the separation to sort through my confusion in light of the new information.

Unexpected insights came. I realized why I had always felt so uncomfortable when my oldest daughter brought boyfriends home without telling me ahead of time: it was a reenactment of the visits from my uncle that set the scene for abuse. A generalized fear of others, which I had not even been aware of carrying, began to crumble. I revised my irrational assumption that all others must be viewed as potentially dangerous.

Thanksgiving was quickly approaching. My younger sister and I had arranged for a family reunion near the beach. Our husbands, our parents, our brother, our youngest sister and her husband, and all the grandchildren would be coming. My uncle would not. He had been dead for years.

The arrangements had been made months before. As the

time grew near, I began to feel anxious about being with the family. I talked about my increasing feelings of vulnerability with the therapist I had just started seeing, and about ways to prepare myself for the family gathering. My younger sister knew, but the others did not. Should I tell everyone? Some? How to tell them? What would their reactions be? Would the disclosure ruin the family holiday?

In a telephone conversation a week or so before Thanksgiving, I told my brother that I too had remembered abuse. His memories had surfaced just a few months earlier, and he was still struggling to put his life back together. Against my wishes, he blurted out the information about my abuse in a meeting with our parents. He told me this by phone just a few days before our family was to get together for the reunion he chose not to attend. I felt furious with my brother but relieved that the dilemma of how to tell my parents was solved. I then called my youngest sister and told her. I did not want to hold any family secrets.

The family gathering was bittersweet for me. It was good to be with everyone, but I felt estranged. Little was said about what everyone knew. That suited me fine. I felt vulnerable yet charged with angry energy as I moved among the family members. I took an active role in seeing that things flowed smoothly at the get-together. I wanted to avoid, above all, awkward silences that made space for open discussions.

I had brought a candle to light at the Thanksgiving dinner we shared. During group picture taking I explained that the candle was to be a symbol of the continuity of our family because centerpieces of candles and flowers have often been a part of our holiday feasts together. For me the candle also signified that something was different about me and my brother, and about our family, since the incest had come to light.

As I lit it, the candle seemed very small and plain. I felt

embarrassed by my insistence on this ritual. Some family members pretended not to see what I was doing. Others commented afterward that they liked my lighting the candle. It was not a satisfying ritual for me. It seemed like something I had to do and stubbornly follow through on, like telling them about the incest.

The flickering of the flame reminded me of my own emotional fragility. Somehow that tiny light only emphasized the darkness I felt creeping in around the edges of my being. As the visit with my family ended, I had the feeling that I was looking at the world through shattered glass. Everything was bright, glistening, and out of kilter.

The Call

Back home, I felt stunned and confused. Getting down to work in therapy helped me realize that I could not deny or diminish what had happened by skating on the thin ice of composure. I had received the call to go below and meet the little girl I had neglected without knowing it.

I created a ritual for that little girl in me. About once a month I found some time alone to scribble the way I had loved to do when I was

My world was shattered by recovered memories.

two or three. I scribbled up and down and back and forth with big arm movements. I used first one hand, then the other. As I scribbled I felt anger, sadness, helplessness, despair, resentment, hope. Sometimes I pressed so hard I ripped the paper, broke the crayon, or scratched the surface of the drawing with my nails. After doing a scribble drawing, I felt tired, calm, and relaxed.

As days passed, powerful feelings of anger, grief, and anxiety tumbled one after another like colored bits of glass in a kaleidoscope. I feared I was losing control, and I was. I began to forget appointments. My work suffered. All this pain just seemed so unfair. I felt victimized a second time by my uncle.

I once read that when the inner balance between who you think you are and who you really are shifts, you go through something like an initiation experience as you find your new equilibrium (Shorter 1988). The change takes you over and shakes you to the core of your being. At such moments, with no intention to do so, you find yourself reenacting the myths that have arisen through aeons of human experience. Perhaps the human search for meaning while in the grip of this mysterious process of psychological change spurred the creation of myths such as those of Inanna, Persephone, and Isis.

One night as I was driving home from work, I thought I saw a huge black hole opening up in the road in front of me. In my mind's eye, I saw myself inside my car, plunging down into the darkness. It was then that I knew I was living out the myth of Persephone. Bound to the pain, anger, disgust, and indignation of my immediate experience, I nonetheless became aware that I was surely not the first to walk this path and that I was not alone in the walk.

I knew myself as hurt, angry, and upset. But there was also within me another part that had always been there, that I became more aware of now. She was a powerful, earthy, motherly aspect of myself that had given rise to She-bear and the she-dog. This part of me was like a wise old woman accustomed to the long view of nature's inexorable cycles, who did not flinch at the necessity of death and who knew the secret of creating a container for new life. She became my inner guide, and her strength held steady the matrix of my life while I, like a trapped insect, struggled to avoid the pain of being held fast at dead center.

Let me be clear: I do not condone what my abuser did. It was wrong, hurtful, and unacceptable. It placed a cloud over my childhood. However, the pain and anger raised up in me by that memory caused a growth spurt that ultimately was to the good because it made possible a closer connection between who I knew myself to be and my deep feminine wisdom, which I conceptualized as the Crone.

My call was a summons from the deeper wisdom within me to grow toward wholeness. My work was to make the wisdom of the Crone part of who I was. My way was through submission to the pain of initiation by darkness wherein I became lost and separated from my former self. And my hope was in making rituals to remind myself that in natural patterns of growth light always follows the time of darkness.

2

The Below

⬛ Winter. The season mirrored my inner state: I felt myself beginning an inexorable slide into darkness. As if the anger, pain, and grief of being abused were not enough, I now had to cope with the process of self-questioning set in motion by the memories rising like new mountains thrusting themselves above the familiar interior landscape of what I thought reality to be, and who I thought myself to be within that reality. My familiar sense of identity was crumbling under the undeniable remembrance of my sexual abuse.

I, like all people, had constructed much of my sense of self from experiences within my family in relationships with those I loved, trusted, and thought I knew. With the realization that one of those relationships had been exploitative, my sense of my place in the family was called into question. I was not sure what was real anymore, what was true, who I was, or whom I could trust. I felt as if the earth had been cut away from underneath my feet.

It was good that I made the connection with my therapist when I did, because as fall passed into winter I began sinking into depression. It became harder and harder to do anything other than what I just had to. I was motivated by high standards of performance, and I put lots of effort into school and work. I was not sleeping very well, fearful that going to sleep would bring up more memories.

Because I was so busy working I had to let go of the house-cleaning, grocery shopping, cooking, and laundry chores that I was accustomed to doing for my family. While I did not particularly like these activities, they were nonetheless part of my former, more leisurely existence before the memories. Not performing these duties meant that yet another aspect of my familiar reality was gone.

About this time I had another dream: I was pushing a door closed. Some force pushed against the door on the other side so that I could not close it. I was frightened. I bolted awake, my heart beating fast.

Strangely, the day following this dream went very well for me, although I was quite tired. I felt free, relaxed, and optimistic. Something had indeed opened up for me. It was mid-December, and I began to move with the flow of holiday activities around me.

The holidays are a time for family gathering, gift giving, and music. I have come to appreciate the Jewish festival of light, Hanukkah, and the pagan traditions celebrating the return of the sun, as well as Christian traditions that rejoice in the birth of the Son. In addition to putting up a Christmas tree, some years earlier I had begun a family celebration on the night of the winter solstice, the beginning of winter. This year the familiar ritual was a reminder of happier times.

On this, the longest night of the year, I gathered all of the old candles in the house and put them into holders. Then I lit them and turned out all the electric lights, filling the house with candlelight. I let the candles burn until they were all used up. This quiet, magical family evening was the heart of our holiday celebration. It provided a warm family time that helped balance the holiday observance that has become so materialistic.

Christmas this year was a time of going through the motions without much pleasure. I was so depressed that looking happy was difficult. I maintained what I hoped was a serene, and therefore unremarkable, front. It felt like a lie, but I did not want to spoil the holiday for those around me. Perhaps reflecting my sense of presenting a false front, I had the following dream:

I was making love with a young man. The front half of his body had been stripped of flesh, so that he was a bare skeleton facing me but appeared to be a regular person from behind. It was a creepy, unsexual experience.

The dream had many levels of meaning for me because I accepted that the man/skeleton was also a symbol of myself. The dream reflected my attempt to look like a living person when I felt half dead inside. It revealed that the man in me—my image of man—was damaged. Yet, the act of making love was a hopeful sign that new life could come from a connection with this injured part of myself. The dream told me also of the necessity of stripping away the flesh, of getting to the basic structure of things, the bones, and of loving the truth of those bones. And the dream presaged the dance with death in which I was to take part during that dark, cold, wet winter.

After Christmas I sank more and more into a state of depression. The model of happy family gatherings around the holidays felt hollow in light of my own scattered family. I missed my two oldest children, now living away from home. I worried that I was burdening my youngest daughter with my neediness. Old wounds were opened as memories of children I had lost began to surface.

My first child was stillborn. She died a week or two before her birth. At the time, her passing did not seem important. I was heavily sedated, never saw her, and returned to life as usual soon after leaving the hospital. Still, I had come to know and love her during the nine months we had been together. I found it unbelievable that I felt so well physically when my heart was dead inside me, but I did not know how to grieve for her.

Several years later I entered therapy when my husband and I were getting a divorce. The pain of losing my firstborn soon surfaced, and I worked for weeks to relieve the burden of guilt, anger, and regret that I carried in her memory. Having done that inner work, it took me by surprise to discover that more than twenty years later I could still feel the pain of her loss so strongly. In some way she had come to symbolize a lost part of myself.

While thoughts of my lost daughter were still on my mind, I dreamed of a rotten log. I could smell the log. It had the rich humus odor of a forest floor. And it seemed all right that a tree had died and become that decaying log. The realization came that the death of this tree was a prelude to new life.

When I awoke, I associated the rotting process of the log to the indigestion I had recently been experiencing. It was as if something were rotting in my belly: dying, returning to the earth. Then I remembered the delivery-room scene when my stillborn daughter had come into the world. I was under anesthetic, but the pain of the forceps delivery awakened me enough to hear conversation between the doctor and nurses. They were not sure they had all of her. She was badly decomposed. Strangely, following this dream and these memories, it seemed to me that the rot, the process of decomposition, was something to value, even to treasure.

The theme of rot was continued in my dreams and interwoven with a sort of sacred marriage:

A homeless man and a reclusive woman met in an art museum. They were dirty, diseased, ugly, and disgusting. They would have been turned out of the museum except that it was a public place and everyone had a right to be there. They cared nothing for the art. They were there only because it was warm.

The man and woman had stumbled upon each other, and somehow a spark ignited between them. They slipped behind a curtain and began making love. Nakedness revealed that their sex organs were enflamed with disease and desire. They were awful to look at, but their mutual attraction would not be denied. Raw, suppurating flesh was split open and torn. The stench of rot was disgusting, yet life shone through the ugliness to infuse the scene with a strange beauty.

The awful embrace of this bizarre couple mirrored my inner state at the time. I felt myself torn apart and my painful places roughly handled. And yet healing in the form of something strange and new coming together within me was hap-

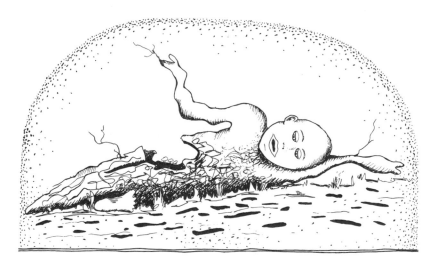

Dream images of a rotting log merged with
memories of my stillborn daughter.

pening even with this excruciating process. My pain was over-ridden by the impulse to birth new life.

Come January the light had completely gone out in my world. I continued my busy work routine, but I had the feeling I was dragging a corpse along with me. I was tired all the time. I spent every spare moment in bed. I cried often when I was driving home from work. I felt like a motherless child and a childless mother. I awoke from yet another dream smelling the pungent odor of a rotting log. Yes, I was now deep in rot, and miserable, but I took comfort in that rotting as a natural process.

My brain was numb. I could not think, write, or even imagine. I forgot appointments with my massage therapist and worried that I would forget an appointment with my therapist. I sometimes awakened bolt upright in a sweat, fearing that I had forgotten to pick up one of the children at day care, a responsibility I had not had for more than ten years. My checking account was a hopeless mess because I forgot to record transactions and could not do the math to balance it. I wrote in my journal:

I feel numb, dead, as if paralyzed. I have lost my voice, like a dumb animal. I am stripped of higher brain functioning such as sensing a future, creating a present with meaning, remembering a past. I have no appetite. I have no inspiration, no excitement, no joy. My days are endured, doing what I am committed to doing.

The long, frightening drive home in the dark should keep me awake, but the boredom lulls me. I fight the temptation to turn the steering wheel and crash into a bridge abutment. It seems that I have no life. Why not end the misery? I am so tired all the time. Always pushing my body to be somewhere, do something.

Where am I? Who am I? Why is this happening to me?

Do I need hormones? A change in schedule? A vacation? Good health? Friends? Whatever I need, right now I feel completely unable to get it. I feel as if I am trapped in the underworld, where the sun never shines, living things don't grow, and children are dead. Even my dreams are no longer a consolation. Last night the dreamscape was as drab and lifeless as waking existence, and I began crying in my sleep. This is an awful time.

Old griefs kept coming out of the closet like dark birds flocking to a kill. In addition to my guilt, grief, and anger about the incest, I was missing my young-adult stepchildren now that they no longer lived with us. The baby I had lost twenty years earlier continued to add her cry to the chorus of lamentations within me. I felt completely hopeless. Yet I kept hold of a tiny thread in the darkness: the belief that life moves in cycles and that this dark time was not forever. My therapist accompanied me on this dark walk through myself. Her quiet witnessing of my process steadied me.

There is little cultural appreciation of the way in which moments of darkness deepen who you are and bring greater spiritual awareness. You are encouraged to stay cheerful, active, and outgoing in order to be socially acceptable. Yet mystics such as Saint John of the Cross (1959) appreciated the subtle transformations of one experiencing a dark night of the soul. "For often, in the midst of these times of aridity and hardship, God communicates to the soul, when it is least expecting it, the purest spiritual sweetness and love, together with a spiritual knowledge" (85–86).

Sometimes our most important insights begin with very mundane imagery: I dreamed that my washing machine broke and made a puddle of water on the floor. I was upset and frantically trying to solve the problem. Then the guidance came to relax, not to worry, to let some time pass and the situation would work itself out.

I awoke and considered the imagery in the dream. The washing machine reminded me of the process of personal growth, shaking things up to make them come clean. The puddle I associated with tears. "Oh, no," I thought to myself, "I hope I don't cry in therapy again today!" Crying was a personal embarrassment. Before all this came up, I had not cried for more than a year.

Of course, I did cry that day in therapy. I wept out the pain of years of heart's labor raising two children not my own, children made anxious and unhappy by their parents' divorce. For fifteen years I had put my best efforts into mothering these children. Now they were gone. This agony, this hurt: somehow it seemed familiar.

Then I remembered my ancestors. Women toiling before me to make a home on the prairie, to birth and bury children. To make marriages with men brutalized by war, addictions, and loneliness. My heritage was to be strong, enduring, silent, accepting, loyal. A bleak, black-and-white existence, a life lived in a place where wind sweeps away the sound of a woman's voice.

Sharing this image with my therapist, she asked quietly, "Is there anything you can bring into that picture to soften it?" I immediately pictured the prairie blooming in wildflowers: blues, oranges, pinks, yellows. It was a comforting thought that helped me stay with the painful self-examination.

My own vulnerability to sexual abuse, my tendency to overwork, not respecting my own limits of strength and emotion, seemed rooted in this stolid pioneer tradition. Habits of being get passed, mother to daughter. And so the vulnerability to abuse is perpetuated. I resolved to change myself, as best I could, to pass on to my daughters, granddaughters, and great-granddaughters a spark of knowledge, an awareness of themselves, perhaps a vantage point from which to judge the challenges they chose to accept and to be less accepting of the demands of others upon them and their bodies.

Even though the rhythm of my life was not changed by this insight, I had a greater sense of having made my own choice to live as I was, and this made a difficult time bearable.

Soon after, as if to remind me of the larger theme of initiation in my inner work, I received a dream that showed me new possibilities for being a crone.

I dreamed I was in a circle of seven or eight people. We were being initiated by a young Native American medicine man. The face of each person was smeared with white clay except for one woman, an elder, whose face was covered with a soft crocheted face mask in pale blue and yellow. It was as if she were so wise and comfortable with the knowledge being shared in the circle that she did not need the clay mask. She claimed the privilege of her age to do something exceptional, to adapt the ritual to her own needs.

In the dream my facial expressions were restricted by the stiff white clay on my face. Perhaps this was a reference to the mask of depression I was wearing during this time, or my attempts to keep a "stiff upper lip." We in the circle looked out at the world through our masks. I thought the masks might also represent a particular view of the world, perhaps even an attitude. The old woman demonstrated that with the seasoning of age one need not be burdened with the rigid point of view shared by younger people. It was possible to take a softer, more comfortable outlook that allowed greater individual freedom while one still remained part of the group. The dream gave me encouragement to see myself as a soft, open-minded, easygoing crone.

Thinking that the *I Ching* might bring some light into my situation, I tossed coins to build the hexagrams. The first was Tui K'an (Oppression or Adversity), counseling that "progress will come through dedication and courage" (Wing 1982; 115). The images of the hexagram included a lake drained of water, words spoken but not heard, and imminent death. The changing-line message suggested that "there exists a frustrating lack of information which stands in the way of progress. All you can do is maintain your composure until things take a promised turn for the better" (168). The message was an uncanny reflection of my recent experience and seemed to affirm my attempt to be patient.

The second hexagram was Li Li (Fire or Synergy), and its image was fire, in the form of the sun. Its message also proved encouraging in that dark time, promising "advantage in correct persistence that results in progress." It advised me to "work toward making the best use of the energy to enact new ideas and further your goals. When energies subside, use the time to rest and gather your strength instead of exhausting yourself with useless struggling" (Wing 1982; 81). Wilhelm (1977) comments that the imagery of this hexagram suggests that "it is early morning and work begins. The mind has been closed to the outside world in sleep; now its connections with the world begin again" (120).

This reading did help to shift my mood to a brighter one. As if in confirmation that I had not been abandoned and that my inner work was bringing about positive changes, I received this dream: I was sitting across the table from a white-haired man with a mustache. He looked very distinguished. I was older, with white hair as well. We were having a romantic dinner. He seemed quite interested in me.

My education for cronedom continued in this pleasant dream. I was given an image of myself as an attractive older woman. The dream presented an alternative to the commonly held notion—apparently my notion—that older men and women do not have sexual interest in each other. My unconscious was challenging yet another of my unexamined assumptions about growing older.

And so I endured the dark time of grieving, surviving on hope kept alive by encouraging dreams now and then and by the shift in mood brought about by the simple rituals I was able to do. I made a ceremony of changing the sheets on my bed. This necessary act became for me a ritual of preparing a comforting sanctuary for my wounded inner child. I stood in the shower and imagined that the water streaming down my back was washing away dark, hurtful stuff from inside me. I went outside at night to stand for a few moments in moonlight. Watching the changing shape of the moon became an acknowledgment of the natural cycles of nature. The prayers I said in honor of the seven directions helped me feel my place in this rhythmic natural flow of change. Every few weeks I pulled out an old basket of oil pastels, the detritus of thirteen-plus years of art therapy. With them I continued my ritual of scribbling.

Doing the scribbles helped me get in touch with my feelings. Sometimes I cried. Sometimes I felt angry and growled or cursed my abuser. After covering the paper with layers of pigment, I scratched the surface with my fingernails. Sometimes I imagined I was scratching him until he cried with pain. Sometimes I imagined I was scratching myself, peeling away all the nasty stuff I did not want to be part of me, part of my past. I took crumbs of color and rubbed them into the paper, finding tiny uncovered areas that would accept them. It was important to me to leave nothing unused.

After scribbling I had a feeling of satisfaction. My arms were tired from the exertion of the large arm motions. I felt as if I had done something. It gave me a feeling of accomplishment. One day the thought came to me as I looked at the dirty, broken pieces of pastels, "When these are all used up, I will be healed." After that the goal of the ritual became to use up everything in the basket.

The concrete actions of this ritual grounded me during a time when the messages from my unconscious became confusing. My dreams were sometimes uplifting, sometimes depressing. They followed a pattern similar to my daytime moods, which had begun to fluctuate between giddy elation and hopeless depression. At times I longed for the predictability of the sodden dysphoria of the previous weeks. One night during this time I dreamed I was an artist:

I was full of energy, intense, living life in the present. I was unconcerned about the thoughts of others. They were fascinated by me and followed me with their eyes. I lay down on a pedestal-like bed, and my lover caressed me and made love to me reverently, like an act of worship.

This dream was followed by more memories of abuse that negated the beauty of the dream. I began to wonder if I would always be haunted by such memories coming when I least expected them. This was a dreary prospect.

Still, the dreams kept coming, and I valued them as messages from the hidden parts of myself. This dream followed soon after my latest recovered memory of abuse. It put a stop to languishing self-pity:

My companions and I were traveling. It seemed we were being followed. We had to kill a woman traveling with us. My companions did her in. She was put in the corner of the bathroom, her knees up under her chin, in a basket like a dog's bed. I felt regret that she had to be killed, and some guilt about it. Someone scattered little plastic game pieces on her. It seemed they were hers. This was done as a small, pathetic gesture of good-bye to the woman. I awoke feeling sad, wondering what she represented.

Perhaps the woman killed off was a part of myself playing

games to get love. The gist of the game was this: if I do something for you, then you owe me your love. It was a dog's life, as evidenced by her burial in a dog's basket. With this realization it seemed as if another self-imposed limit on intimacy melted away, making possible a more spontaneous approach to relationships.

Slowly the change was being wrought within me. Patience and time passing were just as necessary as the inner work of ritual, therapy, journaling, and introspection. As if to drive the point home, I received the following dream:

I was getting a tatoo. It was to alter or cover up an older one I already had somewhere on my back. The tattoo artist was a Chinese man. He worked at a little booth in a large open space where others were also working. I was worried about AIDS, and I asked him, "Are your needles clean?" There was a language barrier and I was not sure whether he understood my question. "Yes, yes," he replied without looking up. I was anxious because his setup did not look very clean. The colors he worked with were red, blue, green, and yellow, the colors of bruises.

The message of the dream seemed to be that the mark of experience upon me was being altered. This change, like getting a tatoo, was painful and even dangerous. Yet I felt I was in the hands of one who, like the crazy bus driver of an earlier dream, knew what was best for me, and that I should accept the process of change. This dream marked the end of the dead time for me. Soon after, I began to experience signs of life, just as the world around me began to bloom with spring colors.

3

The Ascent

With the coming of March I began to feel the stirrings of life again. I lifted my head to see light and color instead of unending darkness and gloom. What a relief! What a mystery: the eternal return of life after cold winter nights. But the rebirth brought its own moments of discomfort. The newness springing to life was unknown and at times frightening.

I dreamed I was in a house, and that fires kept breaking out. I would get scared and work hard with others to put a fire out. Just as I began to relax, another fire would start. Finally someone said that the fire must be traveling behind the wall. I looked closely at the wall and noticed some spots that were browning, a sign that fire was behind it. Someone began bashing a hole in the wall with a heavy tool. As the plaster and lathe of the old walls were stripped away, fire burst from a smoldering spot. I became really scared because I could not see how big the fire might become or how much was hidden behind the wall. I woke up in a panic.

In working with this dream I realized that the imagery of the house on fire had something to do with the frequent hot flashes I was experiencing during this time. I often felt as if I were burning with fever. My mind danced with associations to fire as a natural cleansing phenomenon that was at once destructive, beautiful, and awesome. I was told by a friend that hot flashes were once thought of as the kiss of the goddess. The burning seemed to be linked to my transformation into a fearless woman who could take the heat.

Even though I was feeling less depressed and more energetic, there was still lots of dirty work to do, cleaning out some of the garbage accumulated in my inner world.

I dreamed I was trying to hoist a heavy plastic bag of shit into a garbage can. It was so heavy I could not lift it high enough to drop it into the can. It was my shit. I looked inside and thought I saw some parasites moving in it. I poked around in it and caught glimpses of white, threadlike creatures burrowing into the stuff as my poke disturbed them. I thought, Well, at least I know what they look like so I can find them in a book and identify them. It was a good feeling to get closer to understanding, but disgusting to think of having parasites.

This dream graphically pointed out the unnecessary stuff I had been carrying around. In the dream I tried to get rid of it but could not. Yet examining a small bit of the refuse up close I made a startling discovery of living things in the dead matter. The dream pointed out that there was more to be learned about these parasites. Perhaps they related to the way I had unknowingly kept memories of abuse alive in some hidden part of myself, allowing them to sap my energy. Now it was time to clear out those recesses.

As my depression lifted it was replaced by another feeling: anger. Anger at my abuser raged all the time, adding heat to the hot flashes. I often awoke around 4:00 A.M., then found it hard to go back to sleep. I lay in bed in the dark and burned.

One early morning while lying awake I was struck with a realization. This phase of my life was like *calcinatio*, the alchemical burning process. Alchemy, the ancient science of transformation, was believed to be the process by which base material could be turned into gold by sealing substances tightly in a closed vessel and cooking them with fire. Mine was a psychological transformation through the fire of contained anger. It was burning away what was no longer needed, revealing precious inner treasures made stronger by the process.

My skin suffered from the inner fire. I had itchy red patches from my thighs to my neck that made me irritable. I had told my therapist that I would like to "nail up his hide," referring to my abuser. It seemed that it was *my* hide that was being nailed.

I had taken him inside myself. At first physically, against my will, but later, without my awareness, he became a fixture in my inner world. I was enraged to discover that I was bound to him through having made him part of myself. All these years, unknown to me, he had lurked there, like a parasite sucking energy and skewing my perceptions.

I found that remembering helped me become less controlled by the knot of memories stored under the heading "Uncle K." Anger gave me courage to explore in more detail the experiences of abuse. I worked to look at the broader picture of our family, my place in it, and the events at the time of my abuse. I was helped in this work by my mother, who sent me an album containing pictures and letters Uncle K. had written from boyhood through his World War II service in the Pacific.

The letters he wrote my mother, his older sister, while she was away at college were full of news about school, family, teenage pranks, and ranch work. He was "sweet" on girls and tried hard to "make time" with them at country dances and fairs. Uncle K. was a scrapper and proudly included details of his fights with classmates. The letters never mentioned his mother's chronic poor health or the beatings his father gave him.

Uncle K. did odd jobs around the community and helped with the family ranch operation. His father was never an easy man to get along with, and his explosive temper was often taken out on Uncle K. The conflict between them got more dangerous as Uncle K. honed his fighting skills. The family was relieved, pleased, and proud when he joined the Marines at age nineteen.

It was World War II and Uncle K. left his West Texas home for boot camp at San Diego. Then he was shipped to the South Pacific to serve as an armored tank gunner. Uncle K.'s tank was one of those storming beaches on Guam, Guadalcanal, and Okinawa. Twice he narrowly escaped with his life when the tank he was riding in was destroyed.

The letters Uncle K. wrote to folks back home revealed terrible changes in a young country boy brutalized by combat. He had become numbed to the taking of life. On August 18, 1944, Uncle K. wrote: "It just doesn't bother you a bit to shoot them in the back, legs, or anywhere. All you think about is 'get him, get him.' I thought it would bother me to walk up to a dead Jap, but the only thing that bothers you is the stink. We take a knife and cut their pockets open, pry out their gold teeth and all."

It was soon after this that he had his first psychotic episode. Little was known then about the treatment of post-traumatic stress syndrome. Had he received the therapy available to to-day's soldiers, his life, and mine, might have turned out differently.

Uncle K. made it through the war alive, but he was plagued with mental problems the rest of his life. He was hospitalized several times for depression and paranoid delusions. He was not successful at any of the jobs or businesses he tried.

Uncle K. eventually qualified for veteran's disability, when it became clear that he would be unable to provide for himself.

During his transition from military to civilian life, before it became apparent how sick he was, my parents helped Uncle K. find work. He sometimes spent the night at our place. It was during these visits that Uncle K. molested me. I was five years old.

Before the war Uncle K. was one of my favorite relatives. He was always smiling and fun to play with. He let my brother and me "ride horsey" on his back. For my fourth birthday he gave me a country-western record called "Signed, Sealed, and Delivered." This was not really an appropriate gift for a little girl, but it meant a lot to me. I was heartbroken and cried and cried when I accidentally sat on the record and broke it into half a dozen pieces.

After the war Uncle K. was different. He did not play with us as he used to. Noises startled him. He told mother that he was afraid he might hurt us. After that she asked us not to jump on him any more, and to be quiet when he was around.

In the 1940s awareness of sexual abuse was virtually nonexistent. No doubt it happened, but it certainly was not talked about. My parents failed to notice indications because they never dreamed that such a thing was possible. Sex between adults and children was simply unheard of in the small country town where they grew up.

After one incident of abuse, I had injuries that made it painful for me to walk. I felt ashamed, embarrassed, and unable to communicate what had happened to parts of my body for which I had no words. Obviously something was wrong with me. My mother took me to the doctor, thinking that I had hurt my leg, because I would not walk. The doctor, of course, saw no injuries that needed treatment.

Was Uncle K. a victim too? Many perpetrators are. Did he

victimize others? My brother, and possibly others. Did he feel guilt for what he did? I will never know, although I do feel that in his twisted way he cared about me.

As I worked in therapy, pieces of the puzzle became clear and fell into place. Still, new pieces that had no place to go kept appearing. Like in this dream:

I was being forced to drink some foul bitter liquid from a hose. I refused to swallow the stuff. I spit it out. I woke up spitting onto my pillow. Was this a memory of abuse or was it a metaphor for some other kind of experience? I could not be sure of anything except my distaste for having something forced on me.

One day I decided to do some work with the eczema that continued to plague me. I quickly outlined a picture of my body. The head was small compared with the hips. Arms and legs were cut off like stumps. At first I felt nothing. Then, coloring in the belly where the eczema was worst, I remembered: This is where he touched me. I rubbed hard with the red, scrubbing it into the torso, feeling the burning and itching of my skin. I pushed upward with red, then orange, strokes, covering the breasts and filling in the two stumps of arms.

I burned with rage at my uncle. I relived a feeling of helplessness, like a butterfly pinned to the wall. I picked up purple and colored over the red and orange, then worked on the stumps of legs, lengthening them downward.

I felt heaviness in my thighs as I worked. The same heaviness as when I lay so still, trying not to move under his hand, so puzzled by the sensations of his fingers inside me. When he took his hand away I moved first one leg, then the other, with difficulty. They felt like huge logs. I turned my face away from him, not wanting to see. Then I gathered all the confusion stirred up by his violation and squeezed it into a dark place, still as a stone. There it lay, blanketed by forgetfulness for forty-five years.

In the drawing my back was purple and heavy like my thighs. Scratching the surface of the drawing recalled the surge of pleasure I felt when I scratched my itchy skin. Running my nails over the paper, I imagined that I was scratching my skin. If I could dig deep enough, scratch it to shreds, would I rid myself of his hateful presence in me? If it hurt enough could I forget his touch?

Looking down at my hands I saw dark pigment caked under my fingernails. Slowly, quietly, I felt the hard place of memory of him soften, melt, and begin to drain away. I felt physically lighter, as if I had put down a twenty-pound weight I had been carrying a long time. Then a hot flash surged from the base of my spine to my face. As I burned, I imagined a presence of feminine wisdom whirling around me, searing away the dross of the first half of my life and revealing the strong, proud crone underneath. Without understanding how or why, I knew that the memory of Uncle K. had been swept from my body. In the days that followed, the patches of eczema shrank and finally disappeared altogether. Because this was so, I knew that in the space of those few moments, memory,

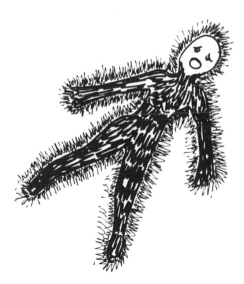

Eczema, hot flashes, and rage made me feel as if I were burning.

emotion, body release, and the symptoms of menopause had converged to create an awesome experience of healing.

My journey continued, and a week later I had another bus dream: I was riding a bus as it rumbled along bumpy streets in a Mexican town. I was glad to have a place to sit down after hours of browsing through little shops. However, I was a bit worried because I did not know where the bus was headed. I wanted to go downtown, but I was not able to communicate with any of the people around me to make that clear. For the moment the ride was nice, the views out my window fascinating, different from anything I had ever seen.

We passed through a neighborhood that was lush and damp. The ancient stones of the sidewalks and buildings were covered with thick, rich green moss, giving everything a soft padded appearance. It was a world like a plush living room armchair. The mist in the air gave sunlight a luminescent glow.

The slow-moving bus took a right turn and we were plunged into quite a different setting. The air was drier. There was no moss. The walls were of natural stone worked in place and had a richly polished, satiny surface that invited touch.

The bus suddenly came to a halt. I looked out the window to see why. Ahead the road narrowed and buildings touched overhead to create a cavelike opening, much too small for the bus—or even a person—to go through. There were ledges carved in the stone near the opening, and they were decorated with strange objects, flowers, and candles.

I asked the driver if we could back up. He agreed to try. Sure enough, we were able to return to the street we had just left. He pulled into the stream of traffic and we continued on our way.

The dream showed that my journey had become less frightening and hectic than it was a few months earlier when I had dreamed of a bus crashing into things and running over people. Even though the driver took the "right" turn, our way was blocked at an opening that seemed too small. The dream points to some sort of difficult passage marked as sacred by the earthy local people. I was to go through, but I was not yet ready. The driver was willing to listen to me and try another direction that was easier, at least for the moment.

The tiny opening in the dream reminded me of the biblical "eye of the needle," a narrow gateway into the city of Jerusalem where camels had to hobble through on their knees. I was also reminded of the Men-an-Tol, an ancient Celtic stone with a rounded opening a little smaller than a person's body. Legend has it that sick people who were passed through the opening in the stone, having their skin scraped as they went, were healed. With the eczema I had just experienced, my skin had surely been well scraped. The impossibly small passage also recalled the birth canal through which a baby miraculously pushes its way. All of these associations made me feel that my rebirthing process would soon reach a climax.

As spring continued to unfold, I began to prepare my garden for flowers. Planting something new and alive had special significance for me this season. I found a reflection of my own inner struggles in the incredible power of tiny, seemingly fragile leaves to push upward into the light from the darkness. The strength of growing things was mine also.

One sunny day I set out for my favorite garden store to buy some plants. During the drive an unexpected empty feeling crept into my abdomen and settled there. In a moment words bubbled up from there: They're gone. The children are gone. A sense of sadness came over me. No more young ones playing in the yard. No more eggs. No more pregnancies. Then the emptiness became a profound quietness, fertile with possibilities. I felt relief to be free of the terrible and wonderful task of childbearing. Flickering thoughts of new possibilities began to take shape.

Just then I was brought back to body awareness by a jittery feeling in my back, chest, arms, legs. It was an insistent throbbing that had driven my body for much of the past two weeks, since I had missed a period. The spells came every half hour or so, awakening me early in the morning and continuing during the day. They reminded me of the pulsing music of minimalist composers. My body felt like an instrument, flashing silent music. The experience was pleasantly stimulating but quite tiring.

I arrived at the nursery feeling somewhat drained by the palpitations. I parked my car near the entrance and stepped inside, surveying what spring had to offer. The place was filled

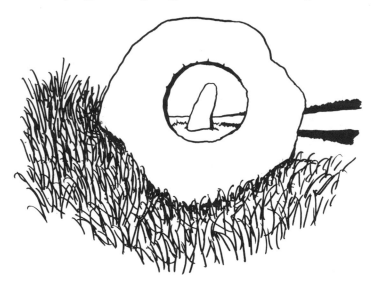

The Men-an-tol, a rock with a hole in it, in Cornwall, England,
is thought to have been used for healing rituals.

with thousands of plants: pink petunias, white nicotiana, yellow iris, red geraniums. The choices were almost overwhelming. I managed to select some colorful petunias and brought them home, but I decided to put off planting until another day.

By the time Easter approached, the rigors of menopausal symptoms, personal growth, and a busy work schedule had made me weary. I felt the need to go on a retreat, and I got in touch with my friend Sister Maurus. Some months earlier she had invited me to come and spend Easter weekend with her and to take part in the religious observances of her Benedictine community. I decided to take her up on the invitation.

I was drawn to experience the Triduum, an ancient Christian ritual of renewal encompassing Easter Sunday and the three holy days preceding it. Easter Triduum celebrates the life/death/rebirth cycle in the passion, death, and resurrection of Jesus. Triduum is the climaxing of the liturgical year. It is thought that Eucharist was celebrated only once a year in the early Christian church, during Easter Triduum. Parts of the ritual even predate Christianity. The Lamentations are rooted in the archaic traditions of Judaism and have been handed down virtually unchanged for thousands of years.

In order to focus my anticipation of the weekend, I cast the *I Ching*. I received Sun Chen (Increase or Benefit), changing to Sun Li (Family). In regard to the hexagram Increase or Benefit, Wilhelm (1981) comments, "The fact that continuous decrease finally leads to a change into its opposite, increase, lies in the course of nature, as can be perceived in the waning and waxing of the moon and in all of the regularly recurring processes of nature" (596). The hexagram affirmed my inner knowing that the wheel of change had begun to move upward toward better times for me. Wing (1982) further described the situation revealed by the hexagram Increase or Benefit:

"Because of the intensity of the benevolent forces surrounding you, you are presented with an excellent opportunity for self-improvement. This is a particularly fortuitous time to discard a self-indulgent attitude or endeavor in order to gain a certain fundamental goodness, a sound foundation, a sense of direction and well-being" (105). Regarding the hexagram of Family, Wilhelm suggests that the situation calls for one to "seek nothing by force, but quietly to confine oneself to the duties at hand" (146). Wing recommended "rely[ing] upon your impulses and natural affections in personal relationships to suggest your appropriate role" (95). I left for the weekend retreat with a happy heart, expecting my experience to be a good one.

The Benedictine tradition of hospitality practiced by this marvelous group of sisters enveloped me in a warm, nurturing milieu, just as the *I Ching* had predicted. I settled into the retreat house in a room by myself. There were about eight of us there for the weekend. The retreat mistress explained that we were simply to blend in with the community and participate in the rituals of prayer and praise alongside them. Following my orientation meeting Thursday afternoon I joined Maurus and her friends for a convivial dinner.

After the meal Maurus guided me into the simple, elegant chapel to a place beside her in the choir. We began singing the meditative Gregorian plainsong that is part of the worship service. I felt a quickening inside me as I blended my voice with those of the other women gathered there. We were celebrating the Eucharist on Holy Thursday, the anniversary of the original Last Supper almost two thousand years ago. The sounds of the timeless chants filled the church and seemed to reach right into my heart to soothe like a lullaby.

Following Mass the consecrated bread remaining on the altar was taken with ceremony into the Chapel of the Reserved Sacrament. There it would be kept for the next day,

Good Friday, for the ritual consecration of bread would not be celebrated then. Maurus led me into the chapel, a tiny dark room where several elderly sisters sat or knelt in prayer. She silently directed me to an empty chair and quietly took a place behind me.

As my eyes adjusted to the darkness, I saw a golden box shaped like a cube, very dense and strong, where the sacred bread had been placed. As I meditated, the thought of the sacramental body of Christ secured there gave rise to a mental image of Christ dwelling within the tabernacle. Then the image transposed, and I became aware of Christ dwelling in me as a spark of the divine that I, like all beings, carry within me. An experience of light gently filled me with warmth.

I felt strength in this inner light, a flame that lived in my body and could not be put out no matter what happened. It gave me energy that lifted me up from my tiredness. I knew now that my innermost being could never be harmed. It was inviolable, protected, just as the sacramental bread was secured by the golden tabernacle. Only I could open and close that inner sanctum.

With these thoughts, broken pieces within me clicked into place and quiet repose rippled through me. Something became all right that had not been right for a long time. A disturbing sense of vulnerability was eased with my realization of an inner, impregnable safeness within me. In this simple, undramatic moment my rebirth was accomplished. I stood up quietly and left the room. That night I slept wonderfully well.

I dreamed of a golden beetle. I was to draw and color it. Then, when the image was complete, it would become a piece of jewelry—a pin perhaps. The next day I looked up the symbol of the beetle in a symbol dictionary. I read that it was a scarab, the Egyptian god of the sun, and that it symbolized resurrection. My dream affirmed the rebirth I had experienced the night before. It also gently pointed out that I had more work to do, since my dream scarab was not finished yet.

Friday was a day of reflection. I walked on the grounds, wrote in my journal, and joined a group for the Stations of the Cross. Evening Mass was held in the darkened chapel stripped of all liturgical decoration. The service was enriched by the chanting of Lamentations. These ancient Hebrew verses gave voice to the howl of a suffering soul.

On Saturday evening in twilight we gathered outside on the steps of the chapel. Each of us held a single candle. A fire was kindled, symbolizing the light of Christ in the world, and the large paschal candle was lit from it. Carrying the candle, a priest led our procession up the steps toward the darkened chapel. At the prescribed moment, candles were lit from the paschal candle he held. The flame was passed along from candle to candle, spilling light down the steps of the chapel until the whole procession was illuminated. Light had once again returned to the children of God, where before there had been only darkness.

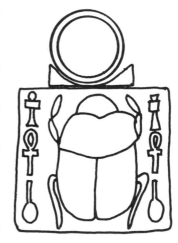

The scarab, a golden beetle, was an Egyptian symbol of rebirth.

The Mass on Sunday morning celebrated the return of light and life after the austere liturgical descent into darkness over the three preceding days. We were joined by many people from the community who had come to be with the sisters for this holy Easter feast. Parents with tiny, angelic children, their cheeks made pink by the springtime weather, crowded into pews next to white-haired elders dressed in their Sunday best. Their colorful outfits contrasted with the pristine white Easter lilies decorating the chapel and filling it with their heady fragrance.

The service was the symbolic conclusion of the whole circular passage of Jesus' descent down into death and darkness and his return again to life and lightness. With my participation in the Triduum, I felt as if I had relived, through rituals, the passage I had just experienced in my own life. The ritual observance of the cycle as a whole helped me understand what I had just lived through. As the Easter service came to an end, celebratory music soared through the lofty space of the chapel and accompanied our buoyant steps out into the spring sunshine.

The Triduum weekend had been all I hoped for and just what I needed. An archetypal celebration of death and rebirth, it had reflected my own personal experience in ways I had not anticipated. I thanked Maurus for her wise and caring midwifery and returned home. I now felt ready to shift energy from inner work toward outer practicalities.

That night I dreamed that I had returned to school to find several children in my class quarantined for tuberculosis. I was in a quandary about whether to work with them or leave the school. I could not tolerate penicillin, and as that was the treatment for TB, I was worried that if I got sick I could not get well for a long time, if at all.

Unlike my dreams of suffering children around the time that memories of abuse surfaced, this dream called into question my staying in an environment with sick children. The need to heal my own inner child had probably contributed to my choice of an elementary school for my counseling practicum site. Now as I became healed, my desire to work with children seemed less compelling. I began to question my intention to work as a school counselor.

Near the end of the school year I attended a conference

with many old friends I had not seen in a while. As we lazed on the beach talking of this and that, I began to get a new vision of what I could do. It was not so different from what I had done before graduate school, but I felt a new excitement about it that told me this was the path with heart for me. I was not to become an employee of any organization. I was to offer my gifts as an independent practitioner to those who came to me seeking healing.

The discovery of my vocation for the second half of life gave me a vision of the crone I wanted to be. This brought to completion an intense time of self-discovery that had seemed like an initiation. During the past few months I had moved through exciting ups and downs while my healing from incest progressed. In the process I had regained a coherent sense of self.

As my psyche had healed itself, my physical body had released bothersome symptoms of eczema, hot flashes, and palpitations. I had gained a deeper understanding of the cyclical changes I had lived through, helped by my participation in ancient rituals built on the same spiraling cycle of change. Life had once again become a delightful pursuit instead of an endurance trial. I knew what I wanted to do. Now it was up to me to put it into action.

4

The New Order

⬤ As summer began it was as if gears were meshing and beginning to turn. I made plans and moved decisively to carry them out. The paralysis of the months before was finally lifted. Around me the world was once again a colorful place where I felt at home. My energy naturally moved from inner work to attending to outer concerns with relationships, home building, and earning a living.

I would spend the next several years bringing into reality the inspirations born of the dark inward times I had just lived through. Even though the focus of my interest shifted to outside myself, I noticed that an awareness of my inner being was now an integral part of my consciousness in a way it never had been before. And in many ways the activities in the outer world were an uncanny reflection of my inner reality.

An example of this reflection was, surprisingly, manifested in an ambitious project to spruce up the appearance of our 130-year-old white farmhouse in the suburbs. I decided to paint the house myself, and I recruited my thirteen-year-old daughter to work with me. Like Demeter and Persephone, my daughter and I had been traveling our own separate journeys for several months. Now, standing next to her scraping and painting through the fragrant Southern mornings, we were reunited. It was a great pleasure to discover the person she had become. Looking up at her perched on a ladder, I realized that she had blossomed into a beautiful young woman. During our golden days together I knew that some part of me was coming into full flower as well.

I made wonderful discoveries in relationship to my husband too. My sorting through my confusion about men had made distance between us. For a while I had been angry at all men, even though I knew intellectually that my husband was not to blame for what had happened to me. Now, as my inner wounds healed, I looked across the dinner table at him one evening and found myself flushed with pleasurable expectation as if it were our first date.

I felt a need to mark the change in things between us. Finding a moment when we were alone, I thanked my husband for his support during the difficult months we had just endured. We slipped our arms around each other and stood close for a peaceful moment. Then we stepped apart and smiled deeply, knowingly, into each other's eyes before getting back to the after-dinner chores.

The inner and outer seemed in harmony in my life. I felt I had regained a sense of the balance lost during my upsetting time of change. Now my dreams reflected that stability. The warm reunion with my family and the healing of inner conflicts were symbolized in this dream of a joyful wedding:

The young bride and groom swept down an ancient curving stone stair in a garden setting. I was in a group of observers at the foot of the stair, and as the bride's full satin dress belled out, we caught a glimpse of red and black shorts. A few moments later the bride and groom ran to a limousine to leave for their honeymoon. They had changed and were now wearing short jogging outfits as if going for a run. As they opened the back door of the limousine, they found a laughing boy child, also dressed in black-and-white athletic shorts and top. He was their son. The boy scooted out through the opposite door, taking the family pet, a dalmatian, with him. The boy, the dog, and a girl, their daughter, danced alongside the big black car as it pulled away. It was a happy, festive, occasion.

The dream showed me that diverse elements of my psyche that had been separated had now been rejoined in a new synthesis. The bride and groom represented the duality of masculine and feminine inner qualities in me brought together in symbolic marriage. The dream suggests that this is a remarriage or a second marriage for the couple, since their children are part of the celebration. Even the family dog shows the marriage of opposites in his black-and-white spotted coat. I do not think it was coincidental that this dream came at a time when my husband and I were renewing our commitment to each other. Like the athletic couple in the dream, we were in good shape for the long run.

Even though the pace of inner change had slowed, there was still much reworking to do. These adjustments were at a more superficial level of identity, and yet they had been set in motion by the deep restructuring of several months earlier. Like ripples on a pond created by a thrown stone, the reverberations in my psyche moved outward in ever more gentle waves.

One of the issues that concerned me was keeping myself safe, a reaction to the feeling of vulnerability brought on by memories of incest. My dreams educated me in very practical techniques for protecting my personal boundaries.

I had been recruited to be an undercover FBI agent responsible for solving difficult criminal cases. This pleased me. In a testing and training situation I was seated in a chair. A man passed very close to me. In a clear voice I asked him not to get so close, and explained my personal boundaries to him in a calm, assertive way. I did not feel intimidated by him. My behavior was praised by the FBI trainers. It was just the sort of response they valued and were seeking in new recruits.

This dream was a rehearsal of appropriate behavior for claiming personal space from men in authority. Like any good training program, it included rewards: the praise of the FBI trainers.

Looked at another way, all the characters in the dream represent parts of me. The FBI agents personified an aspect of myself that admires discipline, tough-mindedness, and high performance. The dream highlighted my need to challenge that part of myself that sometimes demands perfection beyond what is humanly possible.

Keeping a balance between the future-oriented, striving parts of myself and the here-and-now, mindful aspects of myself was more difficult as I became busier with work. Rituals helped me find a middle way, a way to bring the timeless inner reality into harmony with the clock-driven outer time. Creating rituals had grown out of and supported my moving through the darkness. Now rituals anchored me as I stepped into the light.

Amid the activities of homemaking and work, I made time to celebrate the summer solstice. The longest day of the year is the official beginning of summer and an ancient pagan holiday marked with festivals of fire honoring the solar deity. It seemed a fitting time to celebrate my own enlightenment, to take stock, and to deepen my connection with the little piece of earth where I lived. By experiencing the nature of the place where I lived, I hoped to know my natural self better. So, on the evening of the summer solstice, I made myself a place to spend the night outside under the big old trees in my backyard.

I cleaned a circle, dug a small fire pit under the pecan trees, and gathered dead tree branches. As twilight approached I carefully constructed a little tepee of twigs in the pit. It caught fire quickly when I held a match to it. Gradually I added bigger pieces of wood to feed the fire's growing appetite. We had not had rain in a while, so I had buckets of water handy to douse the fire if it started to spread to the dry grass around me.

The fire took on a life of its own, creating a magic circle of light in the darkness. I sat back and gazed into the flames. My thoughts rambled through stories of the people who had lived here farming, hunting, and raising families for generations before me—those who had gathered here around their own fires thousands of years ago. I was abruptly brought back from my revery by the popping of the fire.

The task of burning up all the dead wood I had gathered suddenly became all-important to me. I laid more sticks on the embers, and the flames danced cheerfully around them. I stirred, poked, and prodded the fire for maximum burning efficiency. It was enough then to burn, and with the burning to create light.

At last the fire died down to a pulsating heap of embers. It had been a nice fire, and I tended it carefully to keep it burning steadily. The pile of deadwood had been reduced to glowing rubble. It gave me calm satisfaction to have burned it. What did the deadwood represent for me? The painful past, the anger, or maybe Uncle K. himself. The fire-burning ritual had transformed wood to smoke and somehow lightened a psychological burden as well. The ritual had done its work on a level beyond understanding. I watched the coals glow for an hour or two, and then I went to sleep.

After my solstice fire ritual the fires in my dreams became less dangerous and frightening. Once associated with rage, they now began to take on a different meaning. They seemed related to the physiological process of menopause, to the night sweats and palpitations I still had from time to time, and to the

mixed feelings that are a natural part of any change. I dreamed
I was in the spacious living room of a fifties ranch house. Large
windows looked out on a nice view across meadows. There
was a shallow pan on the floor, filled with something like tissue
paper. It seemed prepared for a ritual fire and I decided to light
it. Once the fire was burning, I began to worry that it might
not be safe, that the fire might get out of control.

Someone came into the room and reassured me that it was
all right, but I still was not convinced. Suddenly I was over-
whelmed with sadness, a feeling of having lost someone I
loved dearly. I began to cry. At first I tried to stop my tears,
but then I just let the tears and sadness come.

The tissue paper brought to mind the sanitary napkins I
had used as an adolescent during my periods. A ritual fire for
burning them seemed to say that I no longer needed them.
Their destruction announced the passing of my youthful,
menstruating self. In the dream I experienced grief I was not
aware of in waking life as I took another step toward becoming my new wisewoman crone self.

Some rituals I had begun earlier in my journey were unfinished, and I felt an urgency to complete them now as a way
to mark my transition. I wanted to create a place honoring
the memory of Glynnis, my stillborn daughter. No memorial
existed for her, and my journey had helped me realize that
without one I had confused her memory with that of my own
wounded child self. I needed a place outside myself where I
could observe her memory. I got to work planning something
special for her.

I selected a space near my studio for a small flower garden.
In the center of this garden spot I placed a sculpture of a
thoughtful little angel seated on a rock. Around her I planted
white flowers that seemed to glow in the dark, especially when
the light of the moon shone on them. Some of the flowers

released their fragrance only after dark. I had made a moon garden for my daughter.

The hard physical labor of preparing the soil, placing the statue, and planting the flowers recalled the effort of giving birth. But this time I had the satisfaction of the outcome I had hoped for. After the labor of birthing my daughter I had come home empty-handed. Now, with the garden, I had succeeded in creating a place for living things that would continue to thrive.

I even found a place in my garden for my scribble drawings. The meditative times I had spent scribbling to use up my dirty, broken oil pastels had produced a pile of drawings. As I looked through them, I saw a graphic record of the many

emotions I had expressed while drawing them. At first sadness and rage were reflected in torn paper and scratched surfaces. Then came sheets where quiet determination was expressed in regular spirals of color.

During the time I was making the drawings, when raw emotion had been succeeded by discernment, I had changed my ritual. Upon examination I had found that some of the oil pastels were worth saving. So I had rubbed the dirty residue from their labels and returned them to my

I created a flower garden to honor the memory of my stillborn daughter.

stock of useful art supplies. I had separated out the wax crayons among the oil pastels and melted them down to make small votive candles. These I would use to bring a depth of meaning to other rituals.

I had sorted through the oil pastels just as I had combed through my memories, assumptions, and beliefs. Some had been worth keeping once they had been cleaned up a little. Others had become part of something completely different. Still others were released because they were no longer useful.

When I had used up the last of the oil pastels I remembered that long ago I had told myself that I would be healed of the wound of incest when this moment came. And so I was. The pain and the rage had tempered into understanding. Although I would never forget, I had been able to forgive Uncle K.

Sitting with the drawings before me I pondered what to do with them. I did not want to keep them, but throwing them in the trash just did not seem to honor what the process had meant to me. Somehow burning them did not seem right either. Burying them appealed to me more. Then I could imagine them rotting and fertilizing new life as they transformed.

I began tearing the colorful drawings into strips, then into small squares. As I worked at destroying what I had created, I was reminded of my firstborn daughter. She had been one of my best creations; and she had been delivered in pieces. Her death had not been of my choosing, and yet I was still sometimes haunted by the feeling that I was responsible. Now, consciously destroying my scribble drawings seemed to help me accept my role in her death without blaming myself. I carried the fragments of paper to the garden and buried them there, tucking each piece gently into the ground as if I were laying my baby to rest.

After bringing closure to these important events with rituals, I felt ready to take my ceremonial work in a different direction. I wanted to make the office where I saw clients a healing place for both them and me. The office is in a building behind our house that was once a garage. It has large old-fashioned windows that look out on a pleasant view of wildflowers, apple trees, and blackberry bushes shaded by huge old pecan trees. I sometimes daydream of living the simple life of a recluse in such a little cottage in the woods.

Now I began making some changes, following an inner voice that seemed to have strong opinions. I rearranged the furniture, brought in a daybed and covered it with a handmade quilt. I found a place for my drum, and hung dried flowers from the rafters. I pulled an old iron wash pot out of the tool shed, placed it near the door, and planted flowers in it. I tucked a basket of children's toys behind my rocking chair. An old table once used for family meals provided a roomy surface for drawing. Without knowing when or how, I began thinking of the place as "hers." Who was "she"?

Several years earlier I had received copies of a publication called *Crone Chronicles*. One month the cover of the magazine featured a picture of a wonderfully eccentric old woman. Seated on a tree stump, gripping a rustic walking stick, she faced the camera with a penetrating gaze that conveyed curiosity, amusement, skepticism, love, wisdom, and joy. Unhampered by any artifice, she had a natural dignity that gave her the sturdy presence of a weathered boulder there in her woodland surroundings.

My office had become hers. I began to think of it as the Crone Cottage. Her tastes guided my choices of things to bring in. When clients were there, she sat quietly in a corner looking like a broom. Sometimes she offered her opinions on things by putting startling thoughts in my head that pointed

This image of an aged crone helped me become acquainted with the wise woman healer within myself. (Photograph by Donald J. Miller, Blackfish Studio, Langley, Wash.)

out something I had overlooked. At other times she simply filled the space with radiant, unconditional love.

I knew that the loving old crone was a part of me, possibly a way of being I was growing into. Simplicity, freedom, and joy seemed the message of her teaching. She was the quiet center of myself that I would spend a lifetime knowing on ever deeper levels. And I knew that my offerings as a healer would flow from my connection to that ancient feminine wisdom within. I realized it was she who had sent the message at the beginning of my journey to "make ritual." And make rituals I had. Yet I wondered: was I to do something more? Then one night I had a dream.

I was in an underground room that was very dark except where lighted by warm glowing candles. The room was arranged something like a church, with rows of chairs facing toward the front, where an altar rail defined an empty square space. I stood in the small congregation of men, all of whom were gay. Several young men were kneeling at the altar rail as if waiting to receive Communion.

The man standing next to me invited me to look at his prayer book with him. The book was an exquisite work of art, beautifully handwritten, illustrated, and decorated. It reminded me of sacred writings produced by medieval monks. He pointed out to me the fine drawings and the attention to detail lavished on the book by its creator. The care and feeling with which the book had been made imbued it with a potent, almost magical, quality.

The book had been bequeathed to the man next to me by its creator, a friend who had died of complications from AIDS. The book was his legacy—a gift of beauty, love, and reverence that would be passed on from friend to friend as an acknowledgment of the thread that connects us all to each other.

The prayer book had been created with love by one who

knew he was dying. And yet this book was a celebration of life, of the undying ability to create extraordinary things that have never been seen before. It celebrated not only his own unique life and gifts, but all life. In creating the prayer book to be passed on to others, the artist acknowledged his place in the unending flow of life from parent to child, from friend to friend, and from loved one to loved one.

The men kneeling at the rail were being initiated into the ritual of the prayer book. After the service they might then receive or create their own prayer books. The prayer book was symbolic of the greater mystery with which they were entrusted: that of the celebration of life through creativity. The ceremony, then, was for healing as well as initiation, because it brought a deeper meaning into the lives of those inducted. My presence in the ceremony was arranged so that I could carry the ritual into my circle of friends and acquaintances.

I woke up after this dream, my mind racing with new possibilities. I began to think of what form such a nontraditional prayer book could take. One could write words backward and read them reflected in a mirror. One could write in circles and turn the book while reading it. Or one could walk in circles while reading. If a group used the same words, they could read aloud together as I had seen in my dream.

After hardly sleeping the rest of the night, I awoke the next day filled with the excitement of creating a prayer book that could address some of my deeply felt convictions about life in a way that more traditional worship cycles did not. The circular path I had traveled into the darkness of depression and back into the light presented itself to me as the model for the book. Inspired by the spiraling continuity of life as I had experienced it, I quickly wrote prayers for twelve steps along the way. I added an opening, a closing, and a refrain to be repeated after each prayer and realized that I had created a litany: a service of reading and response celebrating the Great Round of life, death, and rebirth.

I was astonished by the powerful energy that had come through me and found expression in these words. It seemed as if something valuable had been entrusted to me. I resolved to share the litany with care and respect for its timeless message.

The cycle of prayers became the basis of several rituals I created for groups, beginning with a special church service marking the winter solstice. On that, the longest night of the year, some of us gathered in a simple church sanctuary. Clusters of candles around the room provided light to read by. I had arranged chairs in a circle and placed a verse of the litany under each chair. As we took turns going around the circle and reading the verses aloud, we traveled in ritual space the whole journey from beginning to end and back to the beginning of rebirth.

As synchronicity would have it, people had chosen to sit where the verses gave apt expression to their experience of the moment. Several asked to keep the verses they had read because the words were so meaningful to them. Other groups with whom I used the litany were deeply moved as well. I began to think of ways to offer the litany to a larger group of people.

At the same time that I began to share the litany with others, I felt compelled to fulfill my personal vision of a special prayer book as shown in my dream. The words of the litany had been hastily typed on my computer. Now I wanted to transcribe them into my own beautiful prayer book. After studying examples of the work of medieval scribes, I bought a small hardcover sketchbook and some rich, colorful inks. Then I began work on my prayer book. It was deeply satisfying.

Ideas for sharing the litany and the personal prayer book with a larger group tumbled out of my imagination as I worked: art groups for people wishing to create personal prayer books; conferences structured around the stages of the journey through daily readings of the verses; a book explaining the idea of the Great Round of experience and presenting the litany honoring it.

I had commenced this cycle of my journey with the intention of writing a book on rituals. That first attempt had been an academic discussion of rituals for personal growth that I abandoned when I was pulled deep into myself. The only writing I had done since was in my journal, a desperate attempt to keep my equilibrium by recording dreams and a few vignettes of waking experience. Now, as I looked back over my life during the past two years, I saw that my personal experiences, shared in the proper way, might cast a little light for others on the path. With renewed purpose I began writing again. As work on the book progressed, I was blessed with this dream:

Soup was being stirred in a large pot on a stove, and by watching it, I understood the profound effects of that circling motion in nature and in our psyche too. I saw that the drawing of a circle, whether in sand or stirred in a pot, creates the center even as it defines the circumference. And so it is with us that through our spiraling existence we come to know the true center of our psychic life. Like the contents of a well-stirred soup that are constantly drawn from the edge of the pot to the center, we too are drawn into a quest to touch that center in ourselves.

As I dreamed, the essence of the spiraling flow of life opened before me like a jewel box. I rested quietly in that knowledge for a moment beyond time. Then I noticed that the pot was being stirred by an old woman dressed in black. Her eyes twinkled as she smiled at me, pleased that I understood what she had been trying to teach me.

And what was her teaching? That life is a cycle of turning again and again to revisit our past in the context of our present life. The moving force within the cycling is life itself—that rambunctious, upstart energy that leads, pulls, and pushes us to become one with its joy even as it demands that we submit to its pain. All is in perfect balance, if you but have the eyes to see it. And making ritual helps you see it. At least, that is what the Crone tells me.

5

A Woman's Initiation

Having lived through a time of intense personal growth, I can look back on the experience and see that there was, indeed, a form to it. The pain, chaos, searching, and discovery followed an archetypal pattern. It was a spiraling pathway through initiation. My journey carried me down into the depths of myself and then up and back again full circle, back to the place where I began, but knowing myself to be now changed.

As I moved through my time of initiation I felt my bond with other women growing stronger. Despite our great individual differences, we are alike in that we share the opportunities for growth offered by being born with a woman's body. The stream of life gathers us into a great river whose flow is marked by the passages of menarche, childbirth, and menopause. These physical events alter the way others think of us. We also feel ourselves made different by these occurrences. Responding to the inner directives to reshape our identity, a desire to mark our shift to a new way of being quite naturally emerges.

In tribal societies a woman's changes at puberty, childbirth, and menopause are observed with rituals. The ceremonies clearly mark for all the commencement of the woman's new patterns of participation in tribal life. For example, when a girl in some northern Australian tribes begins to menstruate, she is isolated in a hut for three days. Then the women come and paint her with elaborate ocher designs and adorn her with beautiful things from nature. At dawn the next day the women of the tribe escort her to a freshwater stream and assist her in ritual bathing. Then she is led in procession to the main camp, where she is greeted by all who see her no longer as a girl but as a women (Eliade 1958).

Eliade (1994) maintains that the initiation of a girl "consists in a revelation of the sacrality of women. The girl is ritually prepared to assume her specific mode of being, that is, to become a creatress, and at the same time is taught her responsibilities in society and in the cosmos, responsibilities which, among primitives, are always religious in nature" (42).

Rites of passage support the girl's psychological transformation as well. In seclusion she is separated from all the trappings of her past identity, a ceremonial death that offers her protection while she surrenders past attachments. After a period of introspection to accomplish the renunciation of the old, she is then presented with symbols of her new life. In the receptive state created by her solitude, the encounter with the sacred symbols imprints her new identity just as a stamp leaves its mark on soft wax. By accepting her in her new status, the group also helps the girl see herself as a woman.

The initiation of a girl teaches her the spiritual significance of her power to create new life. She assumes her place performing the everyday tasks of being a householder, a parent, a member of her group, knowing herself as like the divine ancestress who gave life to all. Because of her initiation the ordinary aspects of living are given a deeper spiritual meaning, she is allowed into full participation in the group, and she joins others in upholding the way things are in her group.

A woman's coming to old age, on the other hand, is a transition to a way of being beyond the ordinary daily life prescribed by group customs. The woman becomes an elder, an individual in her own right, when she breaks free of her monthly menses and responsibilities of childbearing. She claims her freedom from the taboos that bind the life of younger women in conformity to their biology and the expectations of the group, and assumes a position of greater authority. She uses the wisdom of her experience in reaching beyond the confines of the family to take a position of honor within the larger group. Phyllis Kaberry (1939) reported this observation of the powerful role taken by older women among the Australian aborigines:

> As the women become older they often assume more authority, become more assertive, tender their advice more frequently and interfere where the activities of any of their kindred are likely to run contrary to the tribal law. On the other hand, when anger mounts high and threatens the peace, even safety of others in the camp, they take the initiative in stemming the disputes and temporarily establishing order again. Amidst the shouting, the barking of dogs, the voice of an old woman will make itself heard above the uproar as she harangues men and women impartially. She has a profounder knowledge and interest in mythology than the average person; she possesses a fund of experience drawn from her journeys over wide regions, her attendance at intertribal meetings and quarrels she has witnessed over marriage, wife-stealing, sorcery, and death. She and other women of her age enjoy a great measure of authority, though this will vary according to assertiveness and temperament. (181–82)

Margaret Mead (1928) reported the respect accorded to older women of Samoa who were recognized as experts in household crafts, herbal medicines, and the ceremonial manufacture of black dye. She also saw older women occupying a place of power greater than that of older men within the household. While not observed with such elaborate rituals as the initiation of girls, the menopause did bring a change in a woman's life in the tribe. Mead observed that among the Samoans "the menopause is marked by some slight temperamental instability, irritability, finickiness about food, a tendency to sudden whims and inexplicable fancies" (193). These behaviors usually subsided by the age of fifty-five, when a woman left heavy work in the fields and began her vocation as a skilled weaver, tapa maker, or midwife.

It had been assumed by anthropologists early in the century that rituals of initiation were limited to nontechnological societies. More recent writers (Stein 1994; Shorter 1988; Stevens 1982) have come to realize, however, that rituals marking important changes stem not only from the needs of the group but also from the inner, psychological impulses of individuals. Even when formal rites of passage are not a part of the culture, individuals find a way to mark their important transitions with some sort of ritual, albeit acted out with little awareness of what they are doing (Douglas 1973). While not formally observed in our culture, rites of passage into adulthood are devised by teenagers for themselves. Like their counterparts in tribal cultures, they wear special clothing and take part in behaviors forbidden to them as children (sex, drugs, and fast cars).

One might consider the medical interventions around menopause as a sort of unconscious ritual marking a woman's transition to the second half of life: the more frequent visits to the temple of healing (gynecologist), where blood sacrifices are made (lab tests), with the prescribed ingestion of special substances borrowed from power animals (estrogen refined from the urine of pregnant mares), during a time when the woman is set apart socially from others by what are considered strange behaviors (moodiness, hot flashes, palpitations).

The passage to menopause is being observed consciously more and more by circles of women, their friends, and their families. For example, one women's group in Florida devised this croning ceremony for themselves. The woman wishing to be "crowned" Crone makes a hat incorporating symbols that are significant to her. Then she makes a list of her accomplishments for which she would like recognition. The list often includes achievements that went unrecognized in the patriarchal scheme of things. With her hat and her list in hand, the woman approaches the group and petitions admittance into the clan of the Crone. She is received and led to a place of honor. The women of the group place their hands upon her as the list of accomplishments is read aloud. The initiate is then crowned with her crone hat and welcomed with hugs by all (Taylor 1992).

Even among individuals not consciously seeking initiation to the second half of life, the psyche itself mandates such an experience. Lionel Corbett (1988) describes the experience of a sixty-year-old woman who resisted growing into old age. Then she had a powerful dream that presented to her a new conceptualization of God, one in which her own aging process was linked with the rejuvenation of the deity. She felt that she had been shown her true purpose for living and growing old. As a result of her initiation experience from the dream she came to know the connection between her individual consciousness and the larger reality. Her experience suggests that there is, in the psyche, a presence of great wisdom that introduces us to our new way of being.

Experience has taught me that such transition is an opportunity to foster a sense of self more congruent with your unique personal qualities. It is a step on a journey whose ultimate goal is conscious acceptance of yourself, body and soul. The travel is not easy because the self you know, your ego, often feels wounded by the changes. This is in the order of things, for it seems that you must become less sure of yourself from time to time in order to make room for the soul. I have found that personal rituals provide a comforting sanctuary and help focus the meaning and significance of these times of transition.

For me and the women I know, menopause is a change that has brought about a major shift in identity. Perhaps this is partly because menopause, the end of fertility, is an undeniable event that presages the great event to come: the end of existence as we know it with death. In reality death is always imminent, but the arrival of menopause demands that attention be paid to your own mortality. You find yourself examining who you are, what you are doing, and whether you are satisfied with your life as it is. For some women this causes little more than a ripple in the pond of being, while for others it brings about a profound reordering of existence.

Menopause challenges a woman to confront the unfinished business of her first fifty years, to release her role as mother, to accept the physical changes in her body, and to make choices about what kind of person she will be for the rest of her life. All this inner work is accompanied by physical symptoms that serve to intensify the change. I have come to think of menopause as an intense heat, something like the fire under a cooking pot, that keeps things bubbling in your psyche until your inner work for this stage of life is well done.

The unfamiliar body sensations of menopause direct your attention back to yourself and the things that concern you. This evaluation of your life past, present, and yet to come is a natural response. It is a journey that deepens your connection to soul, that part of you that is eternal. The journey begins with a wounding, as such journeys often do. You are not alone in your suffering. This quintessential human experience is felt by those around you, as it was by your ancestors at the dawn of human history. You may even find your journey reflected in the ancient myths of Greece, Egypt, and the Middle East.

Many women are reluctant to accept the pain of their menopausal transition, preferring instead to deny the change with measures that purport to prolong youth. This is understandable because at no other time of life is there such a confluence of powerful issues affecting identity. A woman's youth is past. Her children no longer need her in the same way. The working woman faces competition from her younger sisters. Her parents may be dead or incapable of giving her the support they once did.

Looked at in a positive way, menopause also commences a time of greater freedom for a woman: freedom from parental responsibilities, from the need to please the older generation, and from pregnancy, birth, and monthly bleeding. With maturity a woman can become less perfectionistic, more daring, and open to childlike enjoyment of life. Castillejo (1973) describes a visit with a fifty-year-old woman conversing about the bright possibilities in her future. Seated on the lawn among family and friends, the woman emanated vitality. "I have no idea what is going to happen but I am quite sure something is" (152). The woman did in fact become a writer a few years later.

Still, even a woman who is relieved to be set free from the monthly moontime and who looks forward to what is to come may feel a twinge of regret with the passing of the primal flow of blood. Such a familiar part of a woman's existence will be missed. An established routine of self-care focused around the monthly flow is discontinued. The cessation of the body's predictable rhythm is disorienting.

The changes at menopause impact a woman's sense of who she is, what she does, and what is valuable about her as a person. The inner turmoil and unpredictable body changes of this period can seem like an entrance into dark, unknown places betwixt and between. It is an initiation not unlike those practiced in tribal cultures (Van Gennep 1960; Turner 1967). And as with any initiation, the destination is impossible to know, and there are no guarantees about who will arrive on the other side of change.

Therapists who work with women during this late midlife period confirm that a woman's inner changes often follow the same sequence of events identified in tribal initiation rites (Mankowitz 1984; Harding 1976). That is, it is a passage in three stages: first, the stage of isolation, when an individual withdraws from society and gains a sense of connection to the rhythms of nature; second, the trial of separation from all that is familiar, meaningful, and valuable, when one must often endure physical or psychological pain before receiving sacred knowledge; and third, the reentry of the changed person into group life once again, often marked by a ceremony.

Lincoln (1981) sees that the pattern of female initiation is "one of growth, or magnification, an expansion of powers, capabilities, experiences" (104). In the initiation of a girl this magnification is accomplished by sequestering the girl, often in a dark, womblike space, and gradually endowing her with symbolic items that make her a woman, and beyond this a cosmic being. The menopausal rite of passage also accomplishes an intensification of being. A woman relinquishes her connection with cosmos through the primal functions of her body and seeks a new place within the great scheme of things. She must find a role for herself mediated through the new realities of her body. A woman must descend into the dark, chaotic unknown within herself in order to discover that, beneath all the upset, she is cradled in the arms of the dusky goddess who weaves the web of life. Touching this mystery at the center of herself, a woman is initiated into her new way of being.

This journey of self-discovery was made by Rachel, a menopausal woman in analysis (Mankowitz 1984). The stages of her analytical work resembled traditional tribal initiation ceremonies. Entering analysis corresponded to the stage of isolation. The analysis of Rachel's dream images of a burned house, dead babies, and a hall of lost souls was comparable to the time of ordeal in initiation. Rachel confronted the losses of youth, sexual power, and fertility. These were interwoven with the theme of death, particularly the death of the womb, until she reached an impasse where she felt herself trapped "in the center of my own deadness" (71), her no longer fertile womb. Facing her anger and terror, Rachel broke free of the "womb-tomb" and was reborn into a dream space of green things, recalling the third stage of the initiation process, rebirth.

In response to a compelling restlessness around the age of fifty, my friend Elizabeth created an initiation experience for herself. She withdrew from her city life, packed up her artist's supplies, and went to a remote mountain cabin for several weeks. An unexpected winter storm blanketed the mountain with ice and cut off all communication with the outside world. As fierce winds cracked tree branches heavy with frozen sleet, she channeled her emotions into incandescent paintings of the angels and animal spirits supporting her through her dangerous and lonely incubation.

The climax of Elizabeth's initiation came when she left her cabin and plunged deep into the woods over an ice-covered road to an old Cherokee campground. There she built a medicine wheel and placed objects in each of the four directions— stones, flowers, feathers, shells, and such—to represent the old that she was letting go of and the new that she wished to welcome into her life. Elizabeth returned having claimed her place as a creature among creatures within the natural order of things.

Inner Cycles of the Journey

When you accept menopause as a soul journey, you open yourself to an experience that alters your connection with the mystery within and outside yourself. You come to know that healing energy in the world that works through you for your own good, though often in a pattern you cannot see. This energy is generated within you by the Self, a pattern of wholeness that anchors the true center of your personality in the unconscious. Your familiar self, or ego, responds to this inner dynamism of the Self as your identity blossoms within the opportunities presented by outer circumstances.

The Self is rooted in the deep physical processes of the body itself, and messages from the Self to the ego are often transmitted by physical symptoms (Pretat 1994; Mindell 1982). The profound change in the chemistry of a woman's body brought about by menopause quite naturally creates a notable event in the dynamics between Self and ego. The mutual interaction between ego and Self causes the experience of initiation that can accompany menopause. In this natural process that balances the relationship between Self and ego, you may find yourself confronted with powerful images from the unconscious. Your challenge is to surrender to the unconscious contents and reconstruct your ego to accommodate this new information. For your ego this feels like a great sacrifice, like a kind of death, and depression is a natural part of the change. Yet by this sacrifice of treasured attitudes, you find yourself enriched with a stronger, more complex and resilient ego. A more flexible ego increases your ability to receive and to make use of the ancient wisdom of the Self.

The surge of growth around menopause is but one vivid experience of a lifelong pattern created by the dynamic give and take between Self and ego. Cyclical variations in the connection between ego and Self create the fluctuating levels of energy you experience day to day (Edinger 1987). Like the seasons caused by the earth's greater or lesser distances from the sun, the flow of psychic energy to the ego varies according to the quality of its relationship with the Self. Dissonance between the ego and the unconscious pattern of the Self diminishes the energy available to the ego and results in a feeling of alienation. When the ego is in harmony with the Self more energy flows into the ego, creating a feeling of personal power.

This is a cyclical paradigm of personal growth that links moods, emotions, and energy levels with the naturally shifting relationship between Self and ego. It makes a place for the kaleidoscope of feelings from elation to depression that the menopausal woman commonly experiences. While some manic and depressive states are caused by chemical imbalances that require medication, most emotions arise from the process of living, personal growth, and responses to environmental factors. This pattern is especially familiar to women because of the cyclical nature of our hormonal balance. As Ann Ulanov (1971) explains:

> The blood tides of her menstrual cycle and its attendent psychological effects [mean that] at ovulation, a woman's body is receptive and fertile. She may feel then an emotional expansiveness, an abundance of sexual energy, a new potency in her creative ideas and insights. If her ego is not in touch with this phase of the cycle, she often squanders her energy in increased busyness or talkativeness, or perhaps in nervous flirtations. If she is related to what is happening to her body and psyche, this time of the month can give her increased confidence and new certainty in her own capacities. Because this sense of herself is rooted in psychosomatic reality, it does

not lead to inflation or a drive for power but to stabilization, and a real sense of her own strength. At menstruation, when the body passes its blood-food, a woman often feels an in-gathering of her energy and feelings to a deeper center below the threshold of consciousness. If estranged from that center, a woman experiences this phase as a "curse," as moodiness, as oversensitivity and pain and irritability. If she is in accord with herself, this phase can be a time of developing fertile insights, new relationships, or creative possibilities suddenly opened to her during ovulation." (175–76)

The varying flow of psychic energy is a lifelong pattern for men as well as women. Each time we face the beginning of the end of a phase in our life, energy leaves the ego. The periodic withdrawal of psychic energy to deep, archaic levels leaves us feeling depleted and depressed. The cyclical flux of energy is a natural accompaniment to our changing sense of who we are. Jung (1990) described the experience of decreased psychic energy as "a slackening of the tensity of consciousness, which might be compared to a low barometric reading, pre-saging bad weather. The tonus has given way, and this is felt subjectively as listlessness, moroseness, and depression. One no longer has any wish or courage to face the tasks of the day. One feels like lead, because no part of one's body seems willing to move, and this is due to the fact that one no longer has any disposable energy" (119).

While this is a difficult experience to endure, staying with it can be worthwhile. Carotenuto (1986) writes:

> If one has the courage to go *into* the depression (rather than try to escape it through outer distractions), it is precisely this journey within that enriches a person and allows one to face the world with greater awareness. The one who after such an immersion succeeds in remaining in contact with this archaic base—establishing an ongoing relation between the ego and the unconscious—will be in possession of a broader and

more profound self-image. Such a person is no longer an object among things, but a subject—not directed by others, but self-directed. This is the essence of the process Jung calls individuation. (69–70)

Mythic Pathways of Change

Our ancestors knew the experience of initiation by the darkness. The waxing and waning of the moon, the turning of the seasons, and the life cycle of plants educated our ancestors about the patterns of their own lives as well. Eliade (1991a) suggests that their fascination with the changes of the moon may have given rise to conceptions about their own life and death: "The lunar rhythm regularly presents a 'creation' (the new moon), followed by a growth (to full moon), a diminution and a 'death' (the three moonless nights). It was very probably the image of the eternal birth and death of the moon which helped to crystallise the earliest human intuitions about the alternations of Life and Death" (72).

Cultures based on agrarian cultivation found special significance in the life cycle of the seed: the "Great Round of nature, grain above and growing, and seed below and dying to sprout again" (Perera 1981, 21). They saw life, death, and rebirth lived out before them in a spiraling cycle of continuity. Agrarian cultures with a matriarchal goddess tradition considered death a metamorphosis, not the end of life. As Perera explains: "Death was seen as a transformation to which, like the grain to the reaper, the goddess willingly surrenders and over which process she rules" (22).

The ancients passed on their insights in the form of stories about gods and goddesses. The myths of Inanna, Isis, Persephone, and Ariadne served our ancestors as metaphors for this life–death–life cycle. These tales provided symbolic maps of what a human life could be.

Ritual reenactments of the stories of Demeter and Persephone, Dionysis, and Osiris brought these stories alive in the present moment for initiates into the mystery religions of the day. By becoming part of the cycle of life and death dramatized in the lives of gods and goddesses, initiates were given a deeper understanding of their own personal spiritual destiny. Their willing submission to a symbolic death made possible an experience of mystical resurrection (Eliade 1994).

Initiates were inducted into the mysteries of Demeter and Persephone during autumn ceremonies in the Greek town of Eleusis. From ancient poems describing the events in veiled language, Frazer (1950) concludes that candidates for initiation first were told the story of Demeter and Persephone. Then, after several months of preparation, they assembled in Eleusis for their formal initiation. They fasted for nine days, as Demeter had during her desperate search for Persephone. Then they were accompanied at night to a special place where they kept an all-night vigil in silence. Near daybreak the quiet was broken by the ribald jests of their sponsors. Following this the whole group participated in a solemn communion with the deity by

Worshipers join hands to create a sacred circle on this ancient terra-cotta image of a bountiful mother goddess.

drinking barley water, the drink with which Demeter broke
her fast, from a holy chalice.

After their initiation they were allowed to participate in
the heart of the mystery, the reenactment of the myth of Demeter and Persephone. At certain moments throughout the
ritual they were shown symbolic objects: a bone, apples, a mirror, a fan, woolly fleece (Turner 1988), and finally Persephone
herself, personified by a young woman suddenly stepping out
of darkness into the blinding light of a roaring fire burning in
the sacred inner sanctum (Lincoln 1981). A priest proclaimed,
"The strong is born of the strong," a reference to Persephone's
rebirth from confinement in the underworld and, by implica-
tion, to the mystical rebirth of the initiates. The priest then
silently displayed the most venerated object of all, a single ear
of grain resting in a winnowing basket (Kerényi 1967). Initiates found comfort in their relationship with the goddesses and
in the message their story conveys, that of life as an indwelling
force that is transformed but never dies.

Ancient myths provide a useful map for you as well as you
tread the path of life. Sylvia Perera (1981) found in the myth
of Inanna a metaphor for the deathlike psychological transformation of those experiencing important life changes. Inanna's
path down into the darkness, her sacrifice of her royal regalia
at the command of underworld creatures, and her subsequent
return above with the aid of humble little beings, showed the
importance of self-sacrifice in the quest for deep feminine wisdom. Perera goes on to explain:

> The process of initiation in the esoteric and mystical tradi-
> tions in the West involves exploring different modes of con-
> sciousness and rediscovering the experience of unity with
> nature and the cosmos that is inevitably lost through goal-
> directed development. This necessity—for those destined to
> it—forces us to go deep to reclaim modes of consciousness

which are different from the intellectual, "secondary process" levels the West has so well refined. It forces us to the affect-laden, magical dimension and archaic depths that are embodied, ecstatic, and transformative; these depths are pre-verbal, often pre-image, capable of taking us over and shaking us to the core.

Connecting to these levels of consciousness involves a sacrifice of the upper-world aspects of the Self to and for the sake of the dark, different, or altered-state aspects. It means sacrifice to and for the repressed, undifferentiated ground of being with the hope of gaining rebirth with a deeper, resonant awareness. And it means returning with those resonances, adding them to mental-cerebral, ordinary Western consciousness, in order to forge integral consciousness. From this perspective the story of Inanna's descent is the revelation of an initiation ritual, and it is directly relevant to feminine experience today. This myth shows us also how those dark, repressed levels may be raised, and how they may enter conscious life—through emotional upheavals and grief—to radically change conscious energy patterns. (13–15)

I know the path of initiation described by Perera as the Journey. As I walked the path of my journey, traces of women's experiences from long ago presented themselves to me in ancient myths that took on vivid significance in the present. The stories of Persephone, Inanna, Ariadne, and Isis spoke to me. Each of these stories describes, in metaphor, a full cycle of the Great Round of experience that brings about a woman's initiation. All were meaningful to me at certain times during my journey and helped forge a stronger connection between ego and Self.

Persephone's sudden fall into a strange reality resonated with my experience of recovering memories that, in a moment, changed everything about me, my relationships, and my world. Inanna's choice to go into the darkness, there to surrender the accoutrements of identity, to be killed, and to return to life with the assistance of little creatures made from dirt, encouraged me to trust the hidden process in the darkness into which I was moving.

The tireless persevcrence of Isis as she gathered together the torn pieces of her husband's body and revived him so that a new life could be conceived spoke to me in my own work of reclaiming parts of myself, so long ago hurt and forgotten, and bringing them tenderly into the circle of myself. Ariadne's courage in taking a stand apart from her family, leaving her old life behind, and fearlessly pursuing a loving relationship helped me to claim my own truth, and in doing so to move toward, not away, from people. These stories are filled with rich images that speak to every woman who listens with her heart. However, in this discussion of woman's initiation, I will focus on the myth of Persephone because it was her story, more than any other, that shaped my own journey.

The call to begin your journey may be experienced as an intrusion, a rape, a shock, or unpleasant restlessness. A new, and at first unwelcome, awareness in the body may be an awakening that begins a descent that ultimately demands surrender of established ways of being. Events that presage the journey to be traveled could be an illness that demands the sacrifice of your body's wholeness, a divorce, children growing up and leaving home, the loss of a lover, the death of a parent, or the completion of an important job or demanding project. A summons might also be issued by some mysterious directive of the inner world bringing to remembrance long-repressed memories. Or perhaps the natural changes in your body, such as menopause, will open wide the gateway to the dark below. Let us go more deeply into the story of Persephone's initiation to discover the ways her story can inform the steps of your own journey.

6

The Initiation of Persephone

The story of Persephone was brought to my attention by a powerful waking dream in which I saw myself driving head-long into a dark hole in the highway. My journey was, in some ways, a reenactment of this ancient myth. Through it I was introduced to the metaphor of change as initiation by the darkness. And why not? We know that this story was the basis of the Eleusinian mysteries, rituals practiced for a thousand years in order to guide people into a deeper understanding of the flow of life.

I suggest you approach the story of Persephone as if it were your dream. Accept that each and every character represents a small piece of your own totality. Be open to the truths given to you here in the form of metaphor. Let the story bring light to your own journey through the mysterious process of change.

Following the story I will share some of the meaning I found in it for myself. No doubt you will find layers of mean-ing I cannot see in Persephone's story, since what I know is filtered through my own unique experience. Respect your in-sights into this story while remembering that we can never know all there is to know about a story like this that speaks so powerfully from the heart of human experience.

Persephone's Story

The maiden Kore (usually pronounced Kor-eh) was a lovely child, daughter of Zeus and Demeter, the goddess of life and growing things. Unknown to Demeter, her daughter had a secret admirer: Hades, the king of the underworld, dark land of the dead. He was determined to claim Kore for his own. Hades went to Zeus and asked for his daughter's hand. Zeus said nothing and Hades took this as permission.

So it was that on a warm, lazy day the maiden Kore frolicked in a sunny meadow of flowers. She was little more than a child, and not yet capable of discerning danger in such happy places. Gaia lured her on, away from her mother, with ever more beautiful and fragrant flowers, until suddenly Hades caused a huge chasm to open in the earth. Galloping black horses pulled his chariot up through the hole. He seized the maiden,

Hades kidnaps Kore and takes her to the underworld.

raped her, and plunged back beneath the earth holding her tightly next to him. Kore cried out for help, but none came.

Hades made her his queen and gave her the title of Persephone. At first Persephone passed her time in the kingdom of Hades neither eating nor sleeping. Her unhappiness at being forced to endure such a lightless existence caused her to weep endlessly. With time she grew used to her queenly responsibilities, but she was slow to accept her new husband. Her preferred companion in the kingdom below was Hecate, an old woman with ancient powers.

As she came to know Hades, her feelings toward him softened a little. Her crying was replaced by silence. One day, walking in Hades' fruit orchard, she picked a pomegranate. She bit into the strange fruit, but its bitter taste caused her to spit it out. Nonetheless, a few of the seeds remained lodged between her teeth.

While Persephone endured below, all was not well on the earth above. Demeter, her grief-stricken mother, wandered the land looking for her. One day Demeter came upon Hecate and asked her what she had seen that day in the meadow. Hecate reported that she had heard the cries of a girl, "Rape! A rape!" She had hurried to the meadow, but all was silence and emptiness when she arrived.

Demeter then commanded the sun god Helios, who saw everything that happened on the earth below him, to tell her what he had seen that day in the meadow. He replied that he had seen a dark man with no face, driving a horse-drawn chariot, appear from nowhere. The man had seized a girl in the meadow and carried her screaming and struggling with him as he disappeared back into the dark hole. Demeter then knew that her brother Hades was her daughter's abductor.

Upon learning that her daughter was in the land of the dead, Demeter became even more distraught and refused to fulfill her duty as goddess of fertility. Growing things soon withered, and life on earth was threatened. Zeus was notified, and he came quickly to try to persuade her to accept the situation. She refused. Demeter's grieving continued to cast a pall over the land.

When at last Zeus realized that Demeter would not acquiesce to her daughter's marriage, he sent Hermes to fetch the young woman back, on the one condition that she had not tasted the food of the dead. The miserable Persephone had not drunk nor eaten a crust of bread since being abducted, and so Hades was forced to release her. However, just as she was leaving, the gardener appeared and reported that he had seen Persephone taste the flesh of a pomegranate from a tree in Hades' garden. Hades sent the gardener along with Persephone and Hermes to report this information to Zeus.

When she was reunited with her daughter, Demeter was overjoyed. Then, when she heard about the pomegranate seeds, she became more dejected than ever, and restated her vow to curse the land into ruin. In desperation Zeus called in Rhea, the mother of Demeter, Hades, and himself, to help find a solution. Finally, With Rhea's intercession, a compromise was worked out.

The maiden Kore would stay for three months of the year with Hades, reigning as Queen Persephone. The remaining nine months of the year, she would live aboveground with Demeter. It was felt that the world could survive through three months of Demeter's grief. Her time of sadness became known as winter. With her daughter's return, Demeter joyfully restored life to the plant world and spring burst forth. Hecate accompanied Persephone on her return from the underworld and watched to see that the arrangement was fulfilled as agreed upon.

Stages of the Journey

I identified most easily with Persephone, whose rape reminded me of the events in my own life. Like Persephone I fell into darkness as an innocent child. Her abduction into the underworld was reminiscent of my splitting off a part of my child self into some dark hidden recess. Recovering memories of the sad and angry wounded child within me required that I go willingly into my own darkness.

As I worked in therapy, I felt myself being acted upon by natural forces that seemed alien to me. My dream of being a rider on a bus that whipped around like a snake expressed my sense of being carried along in ways I could not understand. The story of Persephone helped me be patient through the dark time of depression, knowing that despite her wounds the girl Kore matured into Persephone, a woman of authority. In some mysterious way, I grew as I worked my way through the shadows. Following months of incubation I found myself stepping into the light, reborn. I saw that my own initiation followed the stages identified by anthropologists in their studies of pretechnological cultures. And I came to know the archetypal pattern of the Great Round circumscribing my journey.

Mine was a passage in four stages that carried me through a cycle of death and rebirth. It began with the Call, a wounding. Then a descent into the painful darkness Below. As light returned to my life, I began climbing upward through the Ascent. Finally I discovered myself reborn in the New Order. This journey is not mine alone. It is one traveled by all who open themselves to change. As I describe each of the steps on this Journey of the Great Round, perhaps you will find yourself along the way.

The Call

 The Call commences with a moment of balance, completion, and fulfillment, like a child's carefree play in a meadow. My call to "make ritual" came when I thought things were fine in my life. The Call announces the imminent disintegration of a familiar way of life. It heralds the disruption of life to be brought about as the ego deconstructs and material from the unconscious rises to awareness through illness, alarming insights, or uninvited disclosures. The Call corresponds to the first stage of traditional initiation rituals, when the initiate is separated from the tribe as recognition of her having left the old ways of being.

With the Call you feel a sense of shocked violation, impending doom, and a desire to stop everything right here to go no further, or better still, to go back to the way things used to be. It was with the futile hope of recapturing a happy past that I brought a candle to my family's Thanksgiving celebration soon after my memories of sexual abuse surfaced. Paradoxically, you may also thrill to the scent of danger in the air, the promise of new freedom, or a strange fascination that draws you onward into the process. The sheer force of contradictory thoughts and feelings places you on a roller-coaster ride of highs and lows.

Like Persephone, you may experience the Call as a rape, a violation of your deepest sense of self. You may be plunged suddenly into darkness, confusion, and loss. Or the Call may come in a more gentle form as an unexplained restlessness, irritation, or longing for you know not what. So it was for my friend Elizabeth, who felt compelled to spend time alone in a snowbound cabin painting, journaling, and doing rituals for the old and new within herself. It may be a summons, naively heeded without understanding the significance of the undertaking. It may begin with a conscious decision that brings about the destruction of familiar ways built on lies. Such a call was heeded by Joan, who filed a sexual harrassment suit against her highly respected boss. Or the Call may come when customary ways of being have simply become dead, empty, or meaningless. Some inner initiative demands that you move, go, change. Whatever brings about the Call, it seems that the whole moral order has collapsed, and a period of mourning is mandated.

The first step is an inexorable slide into chaos. The old ways are shattered, become hollow, or are ripped apart by outside forces. As obscure truths about yourself come to light, you may feel victimized, hurt, and angry. The messages from your unconscious may seem menacing, as I initially interpreted the cramp blocking food in my esophagus. In your terrible suffering, it may seem as if you are suspended over a bottomless black pit or stretched to the breaking point on a cross. The contradiction between who you were and who you are becoming is so great that you may lose all sense of who you are. You may even wonder if you are going insane.

Some poor souls become so distraught that they are tempted by suicide during this difficult time. It is true that something must die, but it is outworn attitudes, not your body, that must be surrendered. If you are troubled by thoughts of hurting yourself, tell someone and get the help you need. Remember that the pain you experience now carves out a space for the joy to come.

The Journey of the Great Round begins with a call to enter into the dark unknown.

As it was with Demeter, your anger during this time of loss may be difficult for those around you. You may be told, "Things have worked out for the best" or "Put it behind you and get on with your life." While these are attempts to be helpful, they do not honor the reality of the emotions that must be experienced before there can be healing. I found release for my anger through scribbling furiously on large pieces of paper. The truth of accepting your emotion, even though uncomfortable, is an important step toward discovering your new self.

Like the maiden Kore, you too may harbor childlike attitudes, untested assumptions, or even repressed memories that block your becoming fully who you could be. Even when the split-off information is forgotten in order to protect yourself from painful truths, it renders your ego vulnerable to an invasion of unconsciousness in the form of bad moods, depression, or unexplainable rages. For instance, a client of mine was blocked from living a full life by the undertow of forgotten terror she had experienced as a child while witnessing the burning of the family home. Your ego is not on firm ground unless it is anchored in truth.

There may even be a part of you that, like Zeus, Persephone's father, allows the darkness to come. Difficult as it is, you may sense that it is ultimately for your good to leave behind a nurturing place established by outer authority. Just as Persephone's separation from her mother brought about her initiation into womanhood, your responding wholeheartedly to the Call can open your pathway to an experience of unfamiliar modes of consciousness whose integration can help you to claim a stronger, more congruent sense of self.

Hades, the dark one, loved the maiden Kore. So it may be that the darkness in you—that which is hidden, forgotten, or repressed—longs for light, to be known and loved by you. The rough ways of Hades are not acceptable in the world above, nor in our reality. Yet viewed metaphorically, he was the necessary agent of change that severed the mother-daughter bond so that the child could become a woman. As

Young-Eisendrath and Wiedemann (1987) point out, without this necessary separation, a woman is bound to relate as either mother or daughter: "She will feel validated or worthy only in terms of providing nurturant care or in terms of being protected" (75).

Marion Woodman (1985) views Hades as symbolic of the dark unknown, the unconscious. In order to fulfill her feminine potential, a woman must become adept at allowing the richness of the unconscious to penetrate her conscious identity. Only in this way can she fulfill her potential for creative work and relationships. "Persephone, if she is to grow up, must be separated from her mother in order to be receptive to the penetration of Hades. A flexible ego can bend and assimilate the fear released by negative memories in the body and in the psyche. It is painful, but it is an unavoidable life experience on the road to psychological maturity" (131). With time you may learn to appreciate the necessity of the dark stranger who wrenches you away from rigid patterns, thus enhancing your own growth toward wholeness.

As you respond to the Call, you may find companionship with those who meant nothing to you before your journey. Relationships are forged with other truth sayers, and those who value being real. Like Persephone, who claimed Hecate as a friend, you may discover a greater appreciation of older women who have walked this path before you. This reflects your growing connection to the ancient feminine power within you, which I think of as the wisdom of the Crone.

You may feel yourself hungry for the natural world. Hiking a mountain trail, swimming naked in a clear ocean inlet, or standing in the moonlight may give you moments of solace. The dependable structure of nature can be a source of comfort while your inner world is in such disarray. Your contact with nature also heightens your awareness of what is real and enduring within yourself and helps you redefine your place in the universe.

The challenge of the Call is to embrace the Journey. To accept the loss and suffering. To brave the terror of the dark unknown. To tolerate the fragmentation that comes with responding to the Call. And to trust in the presence of reality when all that is real seems crazy. It is hard but worthwhile work.

To fail to accept the challenge is to remain stuck in a place of dread, staving off inner and outer threats with personal defenses that become increasingly more rigid, paranoid, and ineffective. Compulsive behaviors may be desperate attempts to protect and preserve the way things were. Addictions of various kinds offer a temporary respite from difficult emotions, but they, too, eventually adumbrate an even more dangerous spiral downward.

The Below

The Below is a place that is nowhere. It is a point of transition between the end of a cycle and the beginning of another. This time in your journey corresponds to the point in traditional initiations when the initiate begins to receive instruction while in isolation from the group. She learns the meaning of sacred objects and their significance in defining the spiritual dimension of her life thereafter.

You will know you are in the Below when you feel like an empty husk with no life left in you. Strangely, your inner life will be disturbingly active. Your dreams will bring you vivid images, sometimes wonderful, sometimes terrifying, night after night. I dreamed of skeletons, corpses, and diseased vagabonds while I was in the Below. Your dreams may also be quite awe inspiring, with a religious, symbolic, or mythic quality that transcends the personal and leaves you deeply moved upon waking (Stein and Stein 1988). Here is an example of such a dream shared with me by a woman I know:

> I was watching an old man in flowing robes as he walked around the edge of a large body of water toward a dock. He stopped as if he had found what he was looking for and bent over an old wooden bucket. Inside the bucket were smooth pebbles and bright jewel stones dredged from beneath the water. Then I became the old man and peered down into the bucket through his eyes. I saw a beautiful ruby carved in the shape of a heart among the stones. I was transfixed by its gorgeous red color glowing there in the bottom of the bucket there at the edge of the water.

Dreams such as this one reveal the germ of your new being yet to be born. The ruby heart in this woman's dream pointed to the transformation of her wounded, broken heart into a gem of great radiance at the center of herself.

Your time in the Below will seem like a sojourn in strange places following your departure from life as you knew it, not yet knowing where, how—or if—you will step back into life again. You may experience a relaxation of tremendous conflicts as you enter the Below. Your ego is drained of energy. Like the eclipsed sun revealing its corona, this debasement of the ego allows you to become aware of internal structures and processes ordinarily overshadowed. Your original wholeness, present at birth and providing the matrix from which your ego grew, shines forth and gives you an instant of clarity. Like Jonah contemplating the pearl in the belly of the whale, you can look back at what was, see ahead to what will be, and sense the profound rightness of all the experiences that brought you to this moment.

This grace-filled interlude can ignite a flame in your soul that never goes out. Like a luminous seed, this insight is folded into the earthy darkness of the unconscious. There you lose sight of it as you sink into the darker depths of the Below. Yet knowing it is planted there can sustain you through the black, timeless time, bound in the underworld.

Your ego is de-structured by the powerful images flowing from the unconscious. Your waking life may reflect this disorganization in bizarre events and harsh new realities when you are least able to cope. Psychic energy is turned inward for the process of re-creating yourself given your new realizations. This time is most often accompanied by depression, numbness, vulnerability, and an aching sense of loss.

Your body can feel heavy, awkward, and strange as you move. Light is unpleasant for your eyes. Illness may sap your energy and force you to linger in the Below. Even though you are exhausted, it may be difficult for you to sleep. Or you may do nothing but sleep. You, like Persephone, may find yourself weeping endlessly as you endure your time Below. You may have no appetite for the foods placed before you. What you do eat may not agree with you. Yet powerful forces are working for you, within you, at this time.

Mental processes are slowed down or even distorted so that you lose your sense of the passage of time. You languish in an eternal dark present. Some of the cues you pick up from your environment are magnified, while others that are important do not even catch your attention. Abstract reasoning, creativity, and even imagining possibilities other than the bleak ones at hand become very difficult. The sense of adventure has died. You hold on tight to survive.

For some this place feels like hell, the cold, frozen wasteland described by Dante and Eliot. Nevertheless, your sojourn in the Below can be a profound spiritual experience that changes your life forever. The mystics know this time as the dark night of the soul and counsel patience to endure the long wait. Imperceptible changes are taking place.

A woman faced with a long recovery from a serious illness described her time in the Below: "At first I just sat around in a state of shock, staring at the wall. There wasn't energy for anything but the special diet and what needed to be done right then to stay alive. Looking back, that was the only way to start . . . to just stare at the wall. Finally, finally my life slowed down enough to let the assumptions that had driven it all those years fall away" (Duerk 1989, 40).

The silent restructuring of the ego has begun. Enriched by night soil from the unconscious, the ego is coming together again in a new way. As with a butterfly growing inside its chrysalis, nothing of this work can be seen, although you may have a sense that there is activity "down there." This is a time of waiting in trust, for there is no hope. It is a time of enduring what seems like a lifetime in purgatory, watching as life passes you by. In reality, you are at the very center of the universe in this experience. Your changes flow from the undying capacity of life itself to create new forms from brokenness.

A part of you, like Demeter, may continue functioning in the land above during your time Below. You, too, may cease your nourishing of those around you. Since much of your energy is focused within, strong-willed determination is required to perform your job, prepare meals, or even keep your clothes clean. To be emotionally available in relationships may be all but impossible.

The Journey will bring out your inner Hecate as well. Hecate was Persephone's companion during her sad time Below. She was also present above, where she gave Demeter support in her search. Your inner Hecate is that part of you which stands in quiet witness to the process you are living through. She represents the archetypal feminine center of being toward which you instinctively move in order to find your true feminine nature. You will discover Hecate at the heart of darkness, presiding over the underground river that receives your tears.

Persephone's initiation was instigated by her encounter with Hades. So you too can expect to confront images of the masculine in your journey Below. This may be a review of your life experiences with men, or it may be an exploration of the inborn image of man that you, like all women, carry as inner ballast to your outward feminine identity. These two areas of concern are not so different as they may seem, because your inner image of man is fleshed out by your experiences with the men in your life. It incorporates the authority of a father, the loyalty of a brother, and the mystery of an uncle. Your inborn image of man is intimately connected to your image of yourself, and just as your self-image shifts at each life transition, so is your inner image of man impacted. As you go through your menopausal passage you may find it necessary to strip away a veneer of masculine attitudes in order to emerge as your true feminine self.

During the time Below you have an opportunity to learn to be kind to and respectful of yourself. To accept limitations on your energy and to make things easier for yourself. Menopause can help you learn to listen to the inner truths of your body, so long unnoticed through years of the youthful body's efficient, carefree functioning. Recognizing and embracing the contradictions of the durable yet fragile beauty of a human body—your woman's body—paradoxically brings the Mystery closer to ken.

At last, slowly, you are released from the tight embrace of the dark womb Below. Before beginning your ascent you move for a while into the light womb of bliss. Here you enjoy the deep rest needed to complete your healing and gather energy for the arduous passage to a new self. Ego consciousness here is diffuse, dreamy, and impersonal. Complete unto yourself, you may wish for nothing so much as time alone to savor the lack of pain.

The Below is described in mythic stories of the goddess as an often painful but ultimately rewarding place of incubation. Even when you feel dead, there is much lively activity within you. As the goddess Persephone had her allies above who worked for her release, so you have aspects of yourself always available to help you through the process. While a part of you feels dismembered, abandoned, or lost, other parts of you are industriously putting things back together in ways you cannot see.

Because of sluggish mental functioning and clumsy physical coordination during your time Below, you are vulnerable to accidents. Making an effort to pay attention to your movements as you go through your daily routine, allowing plenty of time to get where you need to be, and, in general, guarding against overextending your body are wise precautions to take. Clearing your schedule of all but the most essential activities can help you to maintain your balance.

The challenge of the Below is to choose life, to survive, and to keep faith when there seems no reason to. To live on when you have forgotten your quest and life seems like nothing but painful drudgery. To turn inward and accept that change is happening even though you cannot see it. And to take realistic action to support the growth process you are living by journaling, drawing, creating rituals, entering therapy, or staying in touch with a group of understanding people. These connections give you a lifeline to the realm above.

The Ascent

During the Ascent you feel a burst of energy. It is a time of rebirth, of renewal, of finding your footing, albeit tentatively, in a new existence. During your ascent you find out that you are alive, that there is more life to be lived, and that there is a new way to inhabit your existence. The outer facts of your life may have changed a great deal, or changed little. Each discovery is cause for jubilation and a prayer of gratitude.

You can go through a whole day without wanting a nap. Wonderful! You find yourself out walking, marveling at the sunlight and the birds singing, and your body feels light as a feather. Hallelujah! That dish of chicken soup tastes sublime, and the scent of an orange sets your tastebuds dancing. Praise be! Like a person crawling out of a sweat lodge, you blink at the light, steady yourself to stand, and look about you with wonder. You feel young, tender, and vulnerable in your new being.

The Ascent is a heady time of discovery. The old ways are no more. Things change quickly, and form is fluid as new realities begin to take shape. In traditional initiations this time corresponds to the return of the neophyte into community life following her secret instruction apart from the tribe. It is often marked in pretechnological cultures with special ceremonies of rebirth for the initiate that also serve as rituals of renewal for the whole tribe.

Persephone made her ascent with the seeds of a pomegranate in her teeth. Some say that the seeds Persephone tasted even made her pregnant, and that when she returned to the earth she gave birth to Dionysus. Seeds hold the potential for growing something new, so this tells you that Persephone's time in Hades was a wellspring of new life. For a woman making the transition to elder this message has both psychological and cosmic significance. On the personal level you learn that out of the darkness of depression and loss you re-create yourself and discover renewed inspiration. And for you, as it also was for the Greeks, Persephone's return from the darkness to bring forth a divine child reflects the power to birth from within yourself you own enduring spiritual nature. Persephone, the Bringer of Change, teaches you about your immortal soul.

Persephone's ascent began simply enough. She was released and accompanied by Hermes out of the underworld and back to the earth above. However, when it became known that she had tasted a pomegranate, her future became uncertain. Demeter's joy on being reunited with her daughter was dashed with the news that Persephone was bound to the underworld by having taken nourishment there. She feared she must lose her daughter again.

You too may pass through a confusing adventure of highs and lows as your ascent begins. New-won freedoms may seemingly be snatched away as the realities of your situation come to light. The rubble of your former life demands to be faced, seen with clear eyes, and accepted for what it was. Your challenge is to claim that which has value for you now in putting together your life anew.

Deidre was plunged into depression and grief Below when her partner of fifteen years died suddenly. Just as she began her ascent, with feelings of quickening excitement and optimism about her future, she received a huge bill from a creditor that her companion had never told her about. She felt obligated to pay the debt, but it strained her limited economic re-

Persephone's return, as depicted on an Attic red figured vase from about 440 BC. Hermes, guide of souls (*second from left*) leads Persephone (*far left*) from the underworld through a vagina-shaped fissure, signifying her rebirth. Hecate (*second from right*) then leads the girl by torchlight to her waiting mother (*far right*). (After Lincoln, 1981: 83)

sources as a single person. The stress of this change in circumstances challenged her fragile equanimity and forced her to reconsider an idealized memory of her lover.

In the story of Persephone, there were conflicts among the gods and goddesses about how to bring Persephone back. She was now a married woman with responsibilities of rulership. An outside authority had to be brought in to find a solution. Zeus called in his mother, Rhea, and with her help they found an arrangement that all could live with. When transposing this story to your own psyche, this archaic mother goddess figure might represent your unconscious, that part of the psyche which precedes and gives birth to the ego. When you are faced with the difficulties of structuring a new life for yourself within the conflicting demands of the past and what you have learned from your time Below, the guidance of the unconscious in dreams, rituals, synchronicities, and intuitive insights can be vital for achieving the balance you seek.

Mary Ann, a nurse in recovery from alcoholism, had many dreams of walking along a beach near the ocean. This helped her realize her need to be close to water, and she began to pay weekend visits to her favorite coastal island. On one of her visits she happened to notice an advertisement for a nurse in the classified section of the small local newspaper. She was hired and moved as a permanent resident to the place of her dreams.

The goddess Demeter established the rites of the Eleusinian mysteries to celebrate her daughter's return. You, too, may wish to create a special personal ritual to acknowledge your transformative Journey of the Great Round. A friend of mine invited her friends to a dinner party at her house. At each of their places at the table she put a little package containing her note of thanks for the kindnesses each had shown her during her dark time, and a small gift—a polished stone, a pair of earrings, a shell, a coin—that symbolized her hopes for the future of their relationship. After dinner she brought in dessert: her rebirth-day cake, blazing with candles.

Simple actions you can take will help you reconstruct your life, and in so doing restructure your ego. Making a phone call to a friend you have not talked to since your journey began. Learning a new song to sing your joy out loud. Requesting an application for that training program you now know you will take. Activity naturally follows your incubation in the Below. Actions allow you to express your new self, to explore your newfound abilities, and to lay the groundwork for your new order.

Myths describe metaphorically the way in which human beings move into a new sense of self. The dark Below must not be forgotten. Its memory should be carried along on the Ascent and given a place in the New Order. This puts in place a connection between the Above and the Below. That is to say, a new relationship with the unconscious and the powerful center of the psyche residing in the unconscious, the Self, is forged as a result of the encounter with the dark world of the unknown.

Your changes may be disconcerting for loved ones who have weathered the journey with you in the hope that you would soon be your old self again. Because you have changed, your relationships will need adjusting too. Claiming the truth may bring about alienation and even the destruction of some relationships. You awaken to new and exciting possibilities with people who are flexible enough to enter the dance of change with you. Pat and her husband began taking line-dancing lessons as a first step into their new life together. Perhaps you will now find the courage to release those who cannot accept the person you have become, in hopeful expectation of finding a more suitable friends.

You find yourself drawn forward by the urge to found something new, something more in keeping with your true self. You may enter a new relationship with another person. Perhaps you will accept and appreciate yourself more. The "other" to whom you relate may even be an inspiration for something you do, make, or become. Relaxing on the beach with some old friends, I discovered the vocation that was to pull me forward into the future: a reawakened vision of myself as an art therapist.

In the story of Persephone, the Ascent brought about new alliances: the bond between Hades and Persephone was accepted by Demeter; the mother-daughter connection between Demeter and Persephone was renewed; and the friendship of Hecate and Persephone was recognized. The arrangements were given Rhea's blessing, and Hecate assumed special responsibilities as Persephone's ally and guardian of the negotiated settlement. This balancing of relationships and alliances may be experienced in your inner work as satisfying connections being made, an enriched sense of meaning, and comfortable acceptance of yourself as you are.

With Persephone's return the rhythm of the seasons was set in motion. This dynamic growth cycle of dark winter followed by verdant spring and summer did not exist before her time in the Below. She thereafter assumed a new role as the Bringer of Change, the harbinger of rebirth and renewal. In this role Persephone symbolizes the ephemeral passage of form, but at the same time she exemplifies the constancy underlying the process of change. Persephone's movement between the Above and the Below embodies the cyclical rhythms of the Great Round.

Your journey will bring you a new awareness of change. As you move from one experience to another, one feeling to another, you will begin to know the continuity that links all events to each other. Perhaps you can learn to appreciate each moment you are living as one of many gemlike instants strung together like beads of a necklace. Knowing this you can be less disturbed when living through an unpleasant moment. You will see that it has gifts for you that make possible a moment to follow that is more to your liking.

With your ascent the ego has reconstructed itself. New realities have been accepted. Personal identity has re-formed itself stronger than before, although that strength has yet to be explored and fully known. Adjustments in work, relationships, and lifestyle are being made to reflect your new inner reality.

The challenge of the Ascent is to choose one of the many possibilities available to develop into your new order. It is natural to be quite self-absorbed as you consolidate your sense of self and focus on making choices for the next phase of your life. You will likely feel a contentment you have not known in a long time. Pamper yourself as if you were pregnant, for you are nurturing a new self.

The danger of the Ascent is in succumbing to a desire to linger in eternal springtime, to remain ever childlike, with one foot in the realm of the underworld. This leaves you vulnerable to depression, without the drive to make decisions or to take risks, and dependent on the strength of others instead of your own. Your ego is still fluid at this time and you may be tempted to linger on as a fascinating shape shifter, assuming different qualities of being the way a chameleon changes colors. True, it can be an intoxicating existence, but it is, in the end, a lonely one, for relationships do not often thrive with one so elusive.

Once the inner work of restructuring your ego is completed, and your time in ascent draws to a close, blissful tranquillity gives way to startling encounters. You now once again have a point of view with your own opinions, and others will not always agree with you. Emotion intensifies as you are compelled to leave sleepy, pleasant, narcissistic self-involvement behind, without assurance that you will get your needs met in the reality toward which you are moving. Fear of losing your soft existence may give rise to the sense that others are taking it, and thoughts can escalate into paranoia. You may feel angry, alienated, suspicious, and nervous as you look beyond yourself and begin to engage reality in earnest.

What seemed happily settled in your life and relationships may unexpectedly be reopened. The many exciting possibilities you wish to pursue may be overwhelming and suddenly seem out of reach. Feelings of frustration, anger, and despair may return when your way appears to be blocked. However, bubbling underneath is a strengthening tide of excitement, optimism, and energy.

The New Order

O The fluidity of the Ascent is now replaced with strength, stability, and order. The ego is reconstituted, and the new sense of identity is now fleshed out and familiar. The focus of attention is outward as discoveries in the time Below and during the Ascent are shaped into new creations. This is a time of energy, industry, and accomplishment. This stage does not correspond to those identified by anthropologists in traditional initiations. It encompasses the time lived between those important transitions observed by rituals of rebirth and renewal.

The relationship between ego and Self has been strengthened. The ego structure is more in harmony with the Self's pattern of wholeness deeply encoded in the psyche. Therefore the flow of energy between ego and Self is free and impeded only by the essential difference that the ego operates on the personal level of consciousness and the Self on the transpersonal level of the unconscious.

The story of Persephone tells of the importance of maintaining ties with the realm below. That connection to the archetypal realm of the Self gives vitality to the new undertaking. It sets in motion the creativity that sustains life. The power of the Below blesses the new establishment with inspiration.

As you create your new order you may find yourself feeling differently about the dark. Mardi, a gifted playwright of sixty, had abhored waking in the middle of the night because she felt so alone in the dark. As she made use of the creative energy of the New Order, she found that some of her best ideas for writing came during her occasional episodes of insomnia. She began to see the dark she woke to as a collaborator in her work, and after a while she felt grateful for the quiet nocturnal presence that sustained her creativity.

Your sojourn Below, although it was awful to live through, will, in time, be seen as an encounter that left you enriched in many ways. Your experiences have helped you discover new strengths and resources within yourself of which you would have remained unaware without the testing of your time of trials. Having endured initiation by darkness, you have a resonant sense of what is right and the grounding in who you are that gives you sureness, self-confidence, and natural authority. As a wise friend, a beautiful crone of eighty-five, once said: "People used to tell me how to interpret my world. Now I know choice, freedom and power to create within my own images" (Ross 1981, unnumbered pages).

You may feel that you have acquired a new and constant companion on your journey. Your companion is quietly in the background of things, yet ever present. She eases the sense of personal isolation you may experience from time to time. You will discover her wisdom, the wisdom of the Crone, in your growing ability to see through artifice, to assess what is true, and to advocate from that knowing on behalf of yourself and others who need your support. Georgia began a new career as a political activist working on behalf of young children. Perhaps you will find ways to invite your mysterious companion into your life, as I listen to mine when doing my work as a healer. Your new companion is the ego's image of the archetypal Self, the soulful true center of your personality.

You, like Persephone, may need to establish in your life brief visits to the Below in the form of meditation, retreats, or simply alone time in order to maintain a connection with the revitalizing darkness. A woman I know leaves her family for one week a year to attend conferences at a Christian retreat center. Another woman friend has regular meetings with a meditation group. Yet another has organized a women's spirituality group that creates and performs rituals to observe important occasions in the lives of group members. It is necessary to listen carefully to heartfelt desires when building your new order. It is easy to be carried along by enthusiasm and relinquish the time you need in quiet communion with yourself. Remember, you cannot do it all.

As you move further into your new order you find heightened abilities to learn, to plan, and to love. The resolution of inner conflicts frees up enormous energy for all kinds of initiatives. You no longer experience yourself as acted upon but feel you are the one in charge of your own life. You feel good about yourself, powerful, and self-assured. It is not unusual to be somewhat overconfident of your abilities during this time because so much energy is available to the ego.

The resolution of your inner work may be reflected in dreams of marriage, such as mine of an athletic young couple bounding downstairs to a waiting limousine. This dream also brings in something of my experience in the Below and incor-

porates it into the new scene: the limousine, a vehicle for roy-
alty, recalls the chariot in which Hades and Persephone made
their descent. Now, in the festive atmosphere of the dream
wedding, the black automobile carries the bride and groom
forward into their new life together.

You come to the New Order seasoned by the extremes of
experience, and therefore you are not so easily upset by minor
events. Furthermore, you bring with you a vivid sense of the
spiritual world, the timeless reality behind daily life, that gives
you calm balance before the demands of family, work, and
routine. You know what matters to you, and you have the
clear-eyed dedication of Hecate to see that you get it.

In the New Order, you become ready to do, not just to
be. Your solid sense of self allows you to be alone without
feeling lonely. You are actively involved and take pleasure in
working with others to accomplish your goals. As you bring
your inspirations into reality you devise ingenious strategies to
stay true to your
unique vision while
translating it into a
form that will be un-
derstood in the world.

I was told of a mid-
dle-aged woman, di-
vorced by her hus-
band, who found
meaning in the power-
ful spiritual exercise of
drawing mandalas, cir-
cular designs that are
an image of God in
many cultures. She
wanted to share her

The New Order enthrones new ways of being
firmly grounded in the ashes of the old.

discovery with the congregation of her rather conservative Christian church. Instead of calling the drawings by their strange Sanskrit name, she introduced them as "visual prayers," a concept her fellow church members could understand. This made it easier for them to try the experience that meant so much to her. Many of them enjoyed the drawing, and soon it became an accepted activity in Sunday School classes, women's groups, and even family gatherings at the church. The woman had succeeded in sharing with her church community a pearl of great value from her time Below.

The challenge of the New Order is to wear your authority lightly. It may be difficult to accept your newfound powers without becoming puffed up with pride. Remembering what you endured to get to your new place is a way to ground yourself. Knowing the role of mystery in your transformation will remind you that personal pride in accomplishment is not justified.

With your experience of the New Order you have completed a circuit of the Great Round. Having moved in the footsteps of Persephone through the stages of the Great Round, you turn once again to living your life, but with a difference. You experience yourself as deeper and more complex. You will have a greater reverence for nature and her cycles. And you will have a renewed appreciation of loving connections with others. You have witnessed the awe-inspiring power of the psyche to die and be reborn. That which began as an ending has ended as a beginning.

But the Great Round does not stop there. Even as you fulfill the promise of the New Order, you are setting the stage to receive another call from Below. The next time you hear the Call, perhaps you will more easily submit to what is asked of you. The myth of Persephone shows that after her initiation she went willingly into the Below each winter. Her story may continue to be a useful model for us.

Some say Persephone returned to the underworld
each winter to study with Hecate, the crone goddess
with ancient powers.

7

Persephone Enthroned

The Ancient One within me lifted her eyes to the moon. She began the drumbeat and raised her husky voice in a wordless chant as her feet shuffled to the music. Nestled under the Ancient One's robe, the Daughter added her nimble steps to the dance and joined in her grandmother's song. All around us the world fell silent and seemed hushed, waiting.

As I stood in the moonlight, the Ancient, knowing One and the new young Daughter intertwined with me to become one rich being. One woman dancing, circling to the four directions, feeling the earth mother with each sure step, reaching upward to father sky, and holding close the richness at the center for the good of all the people. I was making ritual. The Ancient One, the Crone, was pleased. This ceremony was in her honor. I was welcoming her as part of me and claiming my identity as an elder, a crone, in my own right.

I had emerged from the intense period of growth that had carried me on the Journey of the Great Round, and my life had settled down to a more comfortable pace. It had been two years since the Cramp had stopped me in my tracks to pay attention, to listen with my inner ear. With this, my vision quest here in the very place where She-bear had come to me,

I acknowledged and thanked all who were my teachers during the journey. My dreams, my family, my spirit animals. I gave thanks to the Mystery, which had brought it all to pass so that I could benefit from the teaching I had received.

From the journey I had learned of

- my body, its pain and pleasure as a crucible for soul, and of the changes of menopause as a soul journey;
- my connection with all women, mothers and daughters within and without;
- my eternal, inner feminine, wellspring of strength and meaning;
- the cycles of life, the spiraling of change in unending patterns of dark and light;
- the importance of staying in touch with the dark unknown; and
- the wisdom in keeping a connection with the darkness by creating rituals.

Through the experience of menopause I confronted the prospect of my death and found much life to live. With the painful remembrance of sexual abuse I reclaimed my forgotten inner daughter and made a place in my life for my lost infant daughter. Through the body experiences of menopause—hot flashes and various aches and pains—I experienced a force that was mine, for it clearly resided in my body, and yet it was beyond what I knew as myself. The strange sensations of menopause taught me about balancing physical changes with my own sense of who I was. This was preparation for the second half of life, which is, above all, a challenge to live with change. As a result of my initiation there were parts of me ready to take the plunge into whatever life offered. I had this dream:

I was following an older couple walking along a path. We were equipped with backpacks and walking shoes. With light, confident steps the man and woman moved ahead of me. They did not even slow their pace as the path became a balancing act along a beam that served as a narrow bridge over murky waters. And when the bridge ended before reaching dry land, without a pause or a glance back, the couple dove into the water, backpacks and all, and began swimming toward their destination. I hesitated at the end of the bridge. The couple seemed to be saying, "Whatever the path brings, do what is called for wholeheartedly. You need not be afraid." Then, encouraged by their aplomb, I jumped into the water too.

My experience of initiation by menopause helped me discover the girl and the crone within me and strengthened my feeling of solidarity with all women. The story of Persephone illuminated the reality that as a woman I was both mother and daughter to myself, rebirthing myself in an ongoing cycle of inner growth. Like the maiden Persephone, I became lost to myself during the initiation of the dark Below. Then, like Demeter, I rediscovered my lost self with joy.

Acknowledging the mother within me linked me into the unbroken chain of mothers who birthed me. Owning the daughter within, I became part of the future of all my daughters. This realization joined me in unity with all women, past, present, and future. Taking the long view, I was removed from the limitations of the present moment and given a sense of immortality.

The realization of my unity with all women, growing out of shared experiences such as menopause, mothering, and nurturing daughters, both inner and outer, created respect for other women, and for myself, too. And so the infinite moment of connection with women living, dead, and yet to be born was brought again into the present. Therein I was presented with the opportunity to live from this respect in my relationships with others. And always, like Persephone, I had my friend Hecate, the Crone, looking over my shoulder, seeing that fairness was served.

Through the journey of initiation I discovered the wellspring of my eternal, inner feminine. This part of me wears the face of the wise old woman. I know her also as the Self, archetypal ground of being, soul sustainer, and God within. She is a personal face on the dark unknowable in which my woman's being is rooted. Some say that Hecate was really the ruler of the underworld and that Persephone descended each year to learn from her. Hecate, the ancient goddess of caves, crossroads, and turning points. She is the one who stands behind Demeter and Persephone, who brings together the mother and daughter to complete the trilogy of the ancient goddess: maiden, mother, crone. This same eternal feminine finds her way into life through woman's sexuality, often symbolized as the goddess who comes in many forms. One of her manifestations is the goddess Persephone herself, fully grown and mature in her womanliness.

The three stages in the life of a woman formed the basis for archaic notions of a goddess who manifested herself as a girl, woman, and crone.

We are told that sometime after her first descent into Hades, Persephone took the handsome young Adonis as her lover. She initiated young Adonis into the delights of sexuality. Persephone and her lover were together during her time in Hades each year. This is a metaphorical way of saying that the darkness generates new life. The story has another level of meaning as well, for I found that following my menopausal initiation, I had a greater appreciation of sensuality as a sacred aspect of the eternal feminine. This was brought home to me by a dream that certainly contradicted the view of many in our culture that older women are asexual: I was wearing an exotic costume—a long, flowing, pleated skirt in a lightweight fabric, and a golden belt with sacred images hanging from it. One image hanging down the front was of the goddess. My breasts were bare. I felt sensual and attractive. Two women admired my outfit. One of them adjusted my belt, trying to be helpful, but it was not right. I readjusted it so the goddess image hung down between my thighs. In this dream I felt myself to be a servant, possibly a priestess, of the goddess whose images I wore. I had taken my place in service to the eternal feminine power within conceptualized by the ancients as the goddess.

Through my journey I learned of the cycle of the Great Round, the ceaseless movement between light and dark, life and death, youth and age, action and stillness. I found that a dose of darkness every once in a while helped keep me alive. The waxing and waning cycles of my physical, mental, and creative energy were to be appreciated as the natural course of life. The story of Persephone taught me that this periodic withdrawal of my energy would be followed by a wonderful rebirth, when inspiration would return, seeming to flow out of nowhere. This helped me relax into the acceptance of some slow days among my fast ones. My bringing a sense of life's cycles into the way I live my life was reflected in this dream: I was an adolescent graduating from school. My graduation present was a bicycle named Sleipnir.

Sleipnir, "the Glider," is the name of the Norse god Odin's eight-legged horse. Sleipnir carried Odin between heaven and earth to his many encounters with gods and mortals alike. On Sleipnir, Odin's son rode into the land of the dead, realm of the goddess Hel, and returned safely home. This self-propelled vehicle replaced the buses and cars that had appeared in my earlier dreams. It suggested that I was now equipped to cycle through every level of the Journey from darkness to light.

Through my journey I learned the necessity of keeping a connection with the darkness within myself. I made contact with this rich ground of being by descending into my own suffering and allowing meaning to emerge from the chaos. And so I will go, willingly, again and again into my own darkness. From these encounters I carry with me into my conscious sense of self bits of the darkness I lived in for a while. It becomes part of who I am ever after. But I need not always give myself up completely to the darkness in order to allow it into my conscious existence. I was helped in this realization by another dream: I held a small chunk of whale flesh that still had its gray skin on one side. It reminded me of the pieces of fish my husband cooks on our outdoor grill. I stroked the skin, marveling at how like human skin it was. The rest of the whale was nowhere to be seen.

The dream recalled my time Below, captured in the belly of the whale. Even though the leviathan could not be seen, I felt the awesome power of its presence. I certainly could not have eaten the whole fish, that is, taken in all of the unconscious, but I could hold, and possibly eat, a small portion of it, taking it in as nourishment for myself. The same message of the importance of carefully modulating contact with the primordial power of the unconscious is illustrated in another story of Persephone.

Amor, the son of Venus, fell in love with the mortal Psyche. Venus challenged Psyche to several difficult tasks before she would allow the lovers to be together. For one of the tasks Venus gave Psyche an empty box and told her to go into the underworld and ask Persephone to fill it with her "beauty" so that the aging Venus could rejuvenate herself. Persephone filled the box with death. When Psyche, not knowing this, opened the box to get some of the beauty for herself, she fell into a deep sleep. Only the determination of Amor rescued her. With the help of his mother, Venus, Psyche was made immortal so that she could join her lover on Olympus.

The power of the underworld that is Persephone's to give can both heal and cause death. In small doses it brings beauty, but in overlarge amounts it can wound or even be fatal. Therefore her power must be carefully contained. Hers is the power of the darkness, in psychological terms the unconscious. Just as a container protected mortals from Persephone's power, we have need of protection from the full brunt of the unconscious. That protection is given by rituals.

The rituals I create to accompany my experience of the cycles of growth help bring the great power down to a comprehensible scale that will nourish, not destroy. Gertrude Nelson (1986) tells the story of children at the beach, confronted with the enormity of the ocean, turning their backs on the water and digging a small hole that soon filled with water. They created their own little ocean on a scale they could comprehend. As the tide came in, the seawater swept over their little space. "With a delicious mixture of thrill and horror, they repeatedly rebuilt their walls, and the ocean repeatedly washed them down. Their manageable sea always let in something of the unmanageable. This was a game that they were able to play at for a very long time. For them it was a religious experience. They had created a hole to catch something of the transcendent" (25).

Through the rituals I create to contain my experience of archetypal reality I am able to allow in just a taste of that power, enough to bring beauty, vitality, and meaning into my life. But it is not just for myself that I touch the archetypal realities of the Journey of the Great Round. There is a way in which the inner work that I do—any of us does—contributes to the evolution of consciousness in all humankind. There is an urge within each of us to give expression to our humanness in a way that transcends our individuality, and in so doing to create an opening for "the universal soul that is striving to become conscious in each of us" (Woodman 1985, 184). In the chapters that follow I will share some of the things I have learned about rituals as a container for the soul's Journey of the Great Round.

8

Making Rituals

"Make ritual," the Crone had said, and so I had. Exploring the wisdom ways of Native Americans, I had taken part in sweat lodges, received talking sticks, and made vision quests. Drawn to search out ancient European ritual traditions, I had visited a monastic community and participated in the venerable Christian rites of Easter Triduum. Led by inner knowing I had created my own personal rituals for easing physical pains, healing childhood traumas, and honoring menopause. Under the Crone's guidance I had deepened my knowledge of rituals through my own personal experiences. I would like to share with you what I have learned in the hope that it will be useful to you for creating your own rituals.

Rituals offer a pause to discover meaning. They set apart a moment in time for experiencing the coming together of past, present, and future. Rituals mark transitions and help integrate changes that have happened, are happening, or may happen (Beck and Metrick 1990). They communicate through symbols that convey complicated ideas in a simple, concrete form that can be intuitively understood. Rituals provide an opportunity to create experiences filled with grace, beauty, and significance to enrich your life.

When you create a ritual, you set aside ordinary time and step into sacred time not measured by clocks. The place in which you perform rituals is sacred, or becomes so through your actions. Objects handled during rituals take on symbolic meanings beyond their daily face value. Actions performed there point to mysteries behind what is literally being done.

Within the sanctuary created by a ritual you can bring all that you are. Here you can offer up your brokenness and celebrate your fullness. In ritual space you can know your strengths and weaknesses, your frailties and your potentials, your wounds and your power for healing. Rituals can help you grasp a sense of yourself encompassing the wholeness of your being.

Rituals are metaphorical, communicating in the language of symbols, which can condense many meanings, even contradictory ones, into a harmonious pattern that can be understood intuitively (Langer 1976). Ideas that are contrary when expressed in words can be elegantly brought together in a single symbol. Take, for example, the struggle of Christians to grasp the idea of a god that is three beings in one. Logic tells you that this is impossible. One apple simply cannot be three apples, and the same principle of thought applies to gods. In an attempt to resolve this thorny contradiction through visual symbols, medieval Irish monks developed Celtic knotwork. Their dazzling graphic designs live on in the sacred texts they embellished, which have come to be recognized as some of the world's greatest art treasures.

The symbolic language of rituals speaks to the unconscious as dreams do. And just as your heart races during an exciting dream, so your body is affected by ritual actions. Hearing the steady beat of a drum, your breathing tends to fall into rhythm with it. The quality of consciousness alters during rituals as well. Right brain activity increases, with an attendant heightening of intuition (Lex 1979). This sets the stage for insights, understanding, and new patterns of meaning (Van der Hart 1983).

When you are immersed in the symbolic actions of a ritual, your unconscious responds as if real actions are being taken (Johnson 1986). This makes rituals a powerful medium for expressing what is necessary for healing but difficult to say. Rituals can be a safe container for acting out behaviors symbolically that would be injurious if acted out literally. If, for example, I am angry at someone and I choose not to confront her immediately, my feelings can be expressed in a ritual by tearing or burying or burning something symbolic. This does no harm to me or the person I am angry at, and performing the ritual action satisfies that part of me that desires retribution. I can then direct my energy toward negotiating, healing, and moving on.

Much of the power of rituals comes from the fact that they are realer than real (Eliade 1991b). They reveal an ultimate

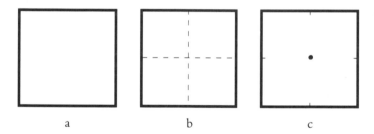

a   b   c

The square, comprising a one-segment grid for the layout of Celtic knotwork (*a*), was overlaid with a two-segment grid created by marking and connecting the midpoints of each side of the square (*b*). For medieval clerics the juxtaposition of a two-segment grid over a one-segment grid illustrated the passage of One to Two. The sum of the overlapping grids (1 + 2 = 3) demonstrated the coexistence of One, Two, and Three, and therefore visually symbolized the Three-in-One, the Trinity (*c*). (After Mehan, 1991: 18) sacred reality that both transcends and generates ordinary reality. The point of interface between sacred and mundane reality is therefore a place of creativity traditionally set aside by human beings as extraordinary. Archaic peoples found this sacred reality in certain mountains, caves, and trees. They wove divine patterns of harmony into the temples, palaces, and cities they built so that the sacred reality could abide there as well. You follow in the footsteps of these ancients when you establish your own ritual space.

Rituals provide a container where fragments of what was can be brought and offered up. They serve as a vessel for welcoming and nurturing the not-yet-become. Rituals create a sanctuary where spirit is welcome, where body is engaged, and where soul is fed by the realness of things. Rituals introduce you to the eternal Now and awaken you to the sacred present in everyday life.

Sometimes rituals just seem to create themselves spontaneously. Such a moment came for me the morning after the birth of my second daughter. Hers had been an arduous drug-free birth at home. She had arrived late in the evening.

The next morning I awoke to find my beautiful daughter sleeping peacefully beside me, the room filled with early-morning sunlight. The intense fragrance of a bouquet of deep red roses sent me into an ecstatic revery. As I held my daughter close, marveling at her delicate perfection, so like a rose herself, wistfulness, delight, happiness, relief, and exhaustion washed together into a burst of joy. Resting in that moment, my daughter and I were gently held within the web of life.

I was moved to honor the benevolence of the universe that had allowed us to survive the birth, and I wanted to mark this quiet moment, poised on the threshold of our life together. The guidance came that I could do this by giving my daughter the name Rose, after the flowers that had sparked my heightened awareness. This, her seldom-spoken middle name, would always be a reminder of the wonderful moment we shared, my daughter and I, resting in the lap of the goddess.

This naming ritual just happened. The sacredness of the moment took me over and I knew what I should do to complete the experience. The ritual simply flowed when inspiration was given expression in the choice of a name that became for me a symbol of life's blessings. Rituals can come into being like this, although most of mine are created with less spontaneity. Meaningful rituals, whether performed on the spur of the moment or planned, are similar in that they are creative, symbolic, and intentional.

During the week of deep introspection imposed by my throat cramp, I performed many rituals. In fact, I chose to see the whole week as a ritual of initiation. By framing my experience as an opportunity to develop spiritual wisdom, I found positive meaning in the events. I could have looked upon the happenings as nothing more than a breakdown in the normal functioning of my body. This would have been frightening, unpleasant, and hard on my body too. Some inner wisdom prompted me to use rituals as a way to establish order and transform my experiences into something from which I could learn. I could not control the cramp, but I could choose my attitude. By directing my thoughts in a way that decreased my anxiety, body processes beyond my conscious control also relaxed.

More than anything I did, directing awareness to the cramp as a time set apart from my ordinary reality transformed an unexpected event into a time of ceremony. My intention to make ritual helped me establish the sacredness of the experience. An intention is simply the goal of the ritual. It can be something like this: "I, Susanne, make ritual for the purpose of learning from the wisdom of my body." (It is efficacious to include your own name when stating an intention.)

When creating a ritual you must first establish a sacred space in which to have it. A sacred space is an opening where the symbolic and timeless can enter into your ordinary existence. By making a place for the unseen powers to be present, you create sacred space that allows the spiritual to enter into your ritual. Places can be made sacred by custom, such as a church or a mountain where people have held sacred worship for a long time. Personal sacred places can be built and dedicated especially to ritual work. For example, a personal altar where you go to pray or meditate is a sacred space. Sacred space can also be created especially for the ritual and done away with when the ritual is concluded.

A sacred space need not be remarkable. Tom Driver (1991) describes walking through a Japanese temple garden where, at a point of divergence in the path, there stood a simple stone with a red string tied around it. The string was very ordinary and so was the stone, and yet the act of encircling the stone with string clearly set this place apart from others and designated it as sacred space. A place becomes sacred when you set it apart in some way from ordinary, daily uses of space.

Sacred space has a different quality than ordinary space. From the earliest times it has been thought to have special benefits—and dangers—for human beings. Many peoples still believe that the pattern of perfection embodied in sacred space can place one in harmony with the true pattern of reality, and that the invisible powers associated with sacred space can bring healing. It is for this reason that pilgrims visit Lourdes, sick people are placed in the center of sand paintings by Navaho medicine men, and devout Buddhists circumambulate the sacred shrine of the Buddha at Sanchi.

Our ancestors prescribed special behaviors for approaching,

honoring, and receiving the beneficent energies of sacred places. However, their actions went far beyond etiquette. They brought into reality in the present moment the living presence of the gods and goddesses. At the same time, our ancestors' rituals offered them protection from the overwhelming intensity of the sacred energy.

While you need not fear the wrath of pagan gods as your ancestors may have, what these ancient practices can teach you is that mystery, even the mystery within yourself that cannot be completely known or understood, demands your respect. The numinous quality of dreams, the uncanny rightness of body symptoms, and the power of visionary art all point to a powerful source within human beings that defies knowing yet communicates a deeper wisdom if you can receive it. To call this shadowy part of you the unconscious is merely to describe it, not explain it. Words such as *higher power, inner knowing,* or even *God within* come closer to describing my experience of this mysterious center. One thing is certain. The unconscious is essentially different from your ordinary, familiar self. When inviting the hidden parts of yourself to be present, you are wise to take an attitude of respect, to create a space that honors the work you are to do, and to acknowledge the presence of mystery.

The way in and out of ritual space is navigated in steps identified by the teachers of wisdom ways the world over. These procedures preserve the boundary between sacred and mundane and guide you into, through, and out of ritual space. You can think of the structure of a ritual as threefold. There is the establishment, or the opening of ritual space. Then there is the ritual action you perform there. Finally, there is the exiting, or closing, of ritual space.

The opening of ritual space can be accomplished by performing an act with the intention of making ceremony. Lighting a candle, burning sweet-smelling herbs, joining hands with others, or drawing a circle on the ground with a stick, colorful beans, or water are a few of the limitless possibilities for opening sacred space. At its most minimal, ritual space can be established by the shift in consciousness brought about by simply focusing awareness on the sacredness of the moment. A silent prayer, a blink, or a nod can suffice to establish sacred space when more elaborate ceremonies are not possible. After a ritual is performed, sacred space is often closed by merely performing in reverse the activities used for opening: the candle is extinguished, incense is allowed to go out, the group joins hands and dances in the opposite direction, or the circle drawn on the ground is rubbed out. A prayer of thanks, a blink, or a nod can close ritual space opened in a like manner.

Simple acts can take on ritual significance with focused intentionality. Putting the ideas and emotions you are experiencing into action through rituals can support your process of personal growth. For example, if you feel yourself on the threshold of something, step through a doorway saying, "I (your name) hereby move toward what will be and release what has been." If you sense yourself at a "jumping-off place," give yourself courage to stick with the process by climbing (safely) onto a chair and jumping to the floor. Finding yourself firmly grounded after your leap can be a kinesthetic message that your fear and anxiety about the change do not signal true danger.

Use your intuition and the images that come to you in dreams, drawings, or reveries when you construct your rituals. For example, a client of mine takes her drawings into ritual space and translates their imagery into sacred dance. Build on the stories and myths that are significant to you. The tales of King Arthur inspired one man to build his own Camelot, a special room where he and his friends could re-create the chi-valric rituals of the Round Table.

Another man I know let his drawing be his ritual on a journey through cancer. He selected his favorite art supplies and put them in his bedroom where he could easily reach them. Then he sat down and drew a design in a circle, a man-dala. (See my book *Creating Mandalas* for more about manda-las). This drawing became the first of many placed in a special folder that he decorated with his power symbols.

For him drawing was a form of prayer. As the moment of his death approached, his mandalas reflected a sublime peace. His ritual of drawing helped him steady himself during a con-fusing time. The drawings collected in the folder became a visual record of his journey treasured by his loved ones after he died.

Performing a Ritual

When I create a ritual, I begin by clarifying my purpose for performing the ritual. Once this is clear I state my intention and usually record it in my journal. For example, the intention to make ritual for addressing problems in my relationship with a co-worker might be something like this: "I, Susanne, make ritual for the purpose of understanding, appreciating, and heal-ing this painful time in relationship to Charles." Stating my intention begins the opening of sacred space for the ritual to follow.

Next I create a physical space for the ritual. I begin by cleaning a place in my house or somewhere secluded out of doors, bringing order and visual harmony to the place. Then, to formally open the space for ritual, I perform some action there. For example, in this instance I put a picture of my co-worker on my altar and placed a flower next to it.

Then I performed the ritual. I wrote an imaginary dialogue with my co-worker to clarify the issues that were causing difficulty, and to get some sense of my part in creating the problem. Placing a pair of shoes opposite me to represent his position, I spoke some key words from my side of the dialogue, saying that he was "arbitrary, uncaring, and stubborn." Next, literally stepping into "his" shoes, I spoke some of the important words outlining his position that I was "invasive, controlling, and ungrateful." I took off the shoes and circled around the sacred space, owning all of these qualities in myself. Then I meditated on the ways in which I was also their opposites: just, caring, flexible, respectful of boundaries, tolerant, and grateful. Finally I took one of my favorite rocks and placed it next to the rose, in front of my co-worker's picture.

After a ritual, I close the sacred space. To end the ritual about my co-worker I rubbed my hands together and clapped them three times. (Three just seemed the right number.) Then I put away the shoes but left the picture, flower, and stone on my altar as a focus for meditation during the next week.

A ritual such as this can be surprisingly effective for shifting your attitude about people and events. It may seem that the ritual has changed things. Actually, the ritual has changed you—your perception of things, your attitude toward them, and therefore your actions. By creating a time and place for honoring all sides of an issue, a ritual can depotentiate habitual patterns, stimulate new thinking, and reveal possibilities you had not thought of before.

It is best to create your rituals using symbols that are meaningful to you. However, sometimes it can be helpful to get ideas for your rituals from what others have done. Traditional rituals can provide good models for your own rituals. For example, moving from an apartment into a house—or from a house into an apartment—may feel like a coming of age, an initiation into a new phase of your life. Looking to the form of a Bar Mitzvah or other traditional adolescent rite of passage can give you ideas for a ritual to mark your own transition. You might arrange a gathering of family and friends in your new home. You could recite a poem to the group, chosen or written especially for the occasion to express your feelings. Consider giving symbolic gifts to those attending. Following the ceremony, all could share in a feast.

Sometimes your challenge may be to bring awareness to the rituals you already perform, rather than to think up new ones. For example, it is customary to send flowers on special occasions. This act of good manners can become a meaningful ritual when you recognize its inherent symbolism. Selecting flowers on the basis of their traditional meanings, you can create a bouquet that sends a message.

In ancient times roses were associated with the goddess Venus and carried blatant sexual connotations. More recently, they have been the attribute of the Virgin Mary. Orchids are thought to suggest male sexuality and potency. Violets are linked with the goddess Aphrodite and express sexual desire. Anemones symbolize sacrifice. Pansies suggest thoughtfulness. The iris, namesake of the Greek goddess of rainbows, represents communication between heaven and earth. Lilies connote the abundant nourishment of the mother goddess (Walker 1988).

The colors of flowers introduce yet another dimension of meaning to your floral arrangement. Red is associated with healing and was once used for disease prevention. White bespeaks purity, spirituality, and virginity. Yellow often signifies consciousness, knowledge, or intelligence. Pink suggests a state of good physical health (Fincher 1991). And so a bouquet of carefully chosen flowers can encapsulate a rich array of meanings that would be ponderous to express in words.

Ritual Cycles

Traditional peoples who live close to the land often build their lives around the seasons that determine the farming, herding, and hunting activities to be performed. Rituals modeled on this yearly cycle arise to assure divine support for the husbandry of the land. Judaism and some Christian faiths preserve this connection to the earth in their liturgical years with rituals that follow a pattern originally established in alignment with rhythms of planting, cultivation, and harvesting. Prayers passed down from our Celtic Christian forebears ask the blessings of Christ on the seasonal chores of harvesting, sheep shearing, and even the making of beer.

In my experience the growth cycle of inner life has its seasons, too, just as the earth does. These seasons have an order of their own that is reminiscent of those created by the dance of earth and sun. It is the passage from dark, wintery beginning through tender spring and rich summer to ripe, autumnal harvest, and then to dark beginning once more. This is the birth, death, and rebirth cycle of your inner life, the Great Round.

Rituals can be a way to hold, celebrate, and make sense of the contradictions of the journey through the Great Round. They provide an outlet for restless energy, a sanctuary for grieving, a forum for claiming personal power. The rituals you create for your journey can support your evolving identity amid the seemingly fragmented aspects of yourself. In this way they can help you fulfill the opportunity for self-knowledge offered by times of great change.

During my journey on the Great Round I discovered that the Call, the Below, the Ascent, and the New Order each require different rituals. The Call was characterized by highs and lows in emotional energy that demanded expression. The low-energy time of the Below called for simpler rituals. Ascent was a time of exploring exciting new possibilities through rituals. I found the high energy time of the New Order gave rise to complex rituals often involving others. Once you identify where you are in the turning of the Great Round, you can create rituals in tune with your needs for that stage of your growing. I have given some suggestions in the following section for rituals that seem appropriate for the Call, the Below, the Ascent, and the New Order of the Great Round.

Rituals for the Great Round

The Call

The Call is a time of ending that begins as you bring completion to something important in your life. You may feel lost, confused, angry, and hurt as you move through your experience of this place. Your familiar way of life is coming to an end. It is often a time of rageful mourning. Rituals can help you express your emotions.

The creation of a personal sacred space, or renewing one already established, seems especially valuable when responding to the call to take up your journey. This might be a secluded place you visit on a walk, a corner in your room, or even a shelf inside a closet. It should be a place where objects that are sacred to you will be safe and undisturbed, yet accessible. Some people like to create a personal talisman they can carry in their purse or pocket. This functions as a portable sacred space and provides a soothing touchstone at moments of distress.

When responding to the Call makes you feel as if you are being broken up inside, put your brokenness into an old ceramic dish, place it inside a pillowcase, and crush it with a hammer. Gather the pieces together and put them in some sort of container: a leather pouch, the bottom of an aquarium, a pot in your garden, or a bowl on your altar. Moving through these activities helps program your acceptance of the process of letting go.

Performed with focus, intention, and caution (in order to avoid accidental injuries), handcrafting activities can be fitting rituals during the Call. Punching a sharp needle through leather when sewing a pouch, pounding clay for making a pot, or carving wood to create a prayer stick can release strong emotions. The actions taken to shape these ritual objects can serve as a metaphor for your felt experience in the midst of the Call. For just as the clay must lose its shape to become a pot, so you must surrender to change in order to discover your authentic self.

Other actions that can be used for creating personal rituals in observance of the Call might include tearing something into pieces (paper, cloth, clay), burning (incense, a torch, a campfire), arranging (bones, a bouquet of dry grasses, or stones), chopping (unwanted garden plants, wood, or vegetables for cooking), or preserving (summer flowers, jelly, applesauce, or chilies).

Sometimes, out of anger, you may wish to give something away that relates to the difficult work at hand. However, giving things away does not seem proper for this early stage in the Journey. The intent of rituals for this time should be to create a strong container and hermetically seal the symbolic elements of your inner work within it so that all is present for the transformation. At the end of the process, after everything has been cooked, so to speak, and all nourishment absorbed from it, objects of the work can be shared, if you wish. They will have been sanctified by your renewal, and they become a very great gift indeed.

The Below

 The Below takes you into darkness. Your hot emotions give way to numbness, grief, and cool detachment. It may seem as if you are viewing events in your life from very far away. Strangely, you may also feel your vision limited to only those things of necessity close at hand. Rituals can sustain you through this difficult time.

Rituals can be a comfort, an act of worship, a step toward acceptance, and a source of stability in the time Below. Since energy is usually low, elaborate rituals, handcrafting activities, or even simply drawing may be too much to ask of yourself. Lighting a candle in your sacred space, saying silent grace before a meal, looking through a kaleidoscope, or holding a small sacred object are effective rituals that take little effort.

As a way to make efficient use of the limited energy available, you might try bringing the special focus of ritual to activities that must be done. For example, changing the sheets on your bed could be approached as a ritual preparation of a place for nurturing those tender parts of yourself that are wounded and in need of rest. Seeing that all the doors and windows are locked in the evening could be viewed as creating a safe, sacred place for yourself to enter the nighttime land of dreaming. An ordinary bath could become a ritual cleansing in preparation for rebirth. One woman I know, a survivor of incest, rubs her heart while standing in the shower and speaks the affirmation "Let my heart be open to the love of the Universe."

A ritual performed by a woman whose relationship with her partner was over helped her honor the incubation period called for by the Below. She gathered up all the objects associated with the relationship—pictures, jewelry, a scarf, letters—and placed them together in a box. Then she wrapped the box with special paper and secured it with twine twisted around the box once for each year she had known her partner. She sat on the floor, holding the box on her lap, and spoke her intention, "I, Jody, release you, Sarah." Then she put the box away in a dark corner of her closet. Speaking the releasing intention and putting the box away helped her accept that the relationship was over.

Actions that might be especially appropriate for creating personal rituals during the Below include burying (a flower bulb, an ear of corn, a doll, an egg), gathering together in a box (legal documents, clothes, seeds), dissolving (salt, earth, colored pigments), collecting in a bottle (tears, holy water, rain from a lightning storm), and cooking (soup, stew, porridge, or ribs).

The Ascent

Your ascent will be an exciting time of new pleasures, burgeoning optimism, and rediscovered talents. You will awaken to the possibilities of life renewed by time spent in darkness. Energy returns and flows in new patterns that reveal who you have become. Rituals can help you sort through the detritus of your journey, identify what is important to you now, and set your direction toward the New Order.

Rituals to help you make your ascent should incorporate the sensory experiences that are so delicious as you savor the end of numbness. For example, you might take a ritual bath by moonlight in warm scented water. Nurturing the new within yourself during your ascent might be enacted by naming a new pet, planting flowers, spending time with children, or making a doll representing some part of yourself you hope to develop more fully. You might arise early to watch the sunrise, light a fire on your outdoor altar, or hang a crystal in your window to catch the sunlight and make rainbows on your walls.

Things tucked away or forgotten during your time Below can now be pulled out, sorted through, and lingered over. Decisions can be made. What is to be kept? What is to be given away? What is to be transformed into something new?

Your time in the Below will have left you with a heightened awareness of the spiritual world. During your Ascent your interest in spiritual matters may draw you to explore rituals in varied religious traditions. For instance, you might become interested in learning more about Egyptian mystery cults, take a class in meditation, or reinterpret holiday celebrations to make them more meaningful for you. Even if you have faithfully maintained your participation in a religious community, you will see the familiar rituals differently since you yourself have changed. What once seemed dead and uninteresting may suddenly take on new life for you. Whatever form it takes, a recognition of your spiritual nature should be honored in some way during your Ascent.

Actions suggested for rituals celebrating the Ascent include eating (colorful, delicious, nutritious foods you loved as a child), dancing (fast, slow, as the spirit moves), singing (old songs, new songs, songs without words), burning (deadwood, old letters, prayers on paper), smelling (flowers, perfumed oils, earthy natural substances), or touching (skin, feathers, trees covered with moss).

The New Order

The New Order brings you into your own as the person you have become. A clear sense of yourself helps you mobilize energy for the accomplishment of your work. Personal power is at a zenith as you move comfortably through the demands and opportunities life presents to you. Rituals balance symbols of the fullness of this time with reminders of the other places you have traveled in your journey.

Rituals of the New Order incorporate references to the complete growth cycle of the Great Round. These include ceremonies that speak of founding the new on the ashes of the old. Old papers, clothing, drawings, flowers, or photographs might be torn or cut and pasted to create something new (a quilt, a collage, or a basket of potpourri). Objects that carry significance might be placed in the bottom of a hole and a new tree planted on top of them. A giveaway of unwanted things from your journey could be made part of a potluck celebration with friends.

By weaving together symbols of the opposites, rituals provide grounding during what is naturally a heady time. Some of the elements traditionally worked with in rituals honoring the opposites are male and female, young and old, dark and light, birth and death, fire and water, earth and air. Examples of rituals that metaphorically balance the opposites include renewing marriage vows, consciously putting on a pair of mismatched earrings, dancing a waltz with your partner, or simply placing black and white objects of some sort side by side on a bookshelf. If you attend a full-moon circle you could suggest that circle members bring symbols of something they are not, to place before themselves. As the talking stick is passed, the members can explain their symbol and what it means to them.

Part of a ritual created for a group of women celebrating the New Year brought together symbols of the old year's experiences and symbols of the year to be. After the ritual space was opened, each woman was invited to think over the past year's experiences and write on a piece of paper something from it in need of release or transformation. The women then gathered in a circle around a fire. When they were ready to, they stepped forward and placed their pieces of paper in the fire. As the women watched the paper burn, they began to stamp their feet and chant. Then, accompanied by drumming and more chanting, each woman was invited to step over a broom laid on the floor, to mark her entrance into a new phase of her life. Once across the threshold she was given an unlit candle to symbolize the potential of the year to come.

When all the women had stepped over the broom, the

group gathered again in a circle to listen to a mythic story of creation, to take turns reading prayers, and to write a word describing "what you are open to receive this year" on a drawing they would take home with them. Then a candle was lit from the center fire, and the light was passed from candle to candle around the circle as the women sang. To close the ritual space, the women held their candles toward the center, then spiraled out of the circle and extinguished their candles. (This ritual was created by the author and Merry Black, Ph.D.)

Other rituals you might perform on your own could include the renewal of your sacred space with an arrangement of flowers or objects that give a place of honor to something that reminds you of your dark time and celebrates your present joy as well. You might buy a special piece of jewelry with fiery gems created in the great heat and pressure of the earth to symbolize the wonderful, though painful, transformation that has taken place inside you. You might even arrange a pilgrimage to a place you have come to realize is quite important to you. Creating something new that honors the arc of your journey through change is fitting ritual work. In celebration of my own new order I wrote prayers for twelve stages along the journey I had just traveled. These prayers became the Litany of the Great Round.

The Litany of the Great Round

The Great Round is a spiraling cycle of growth, change, and transformation that has been intuitively accepted as a paradigm for the unfolding of life since ancient times. It probably grew out of the human fascination with the waxing and waning of the moon and the closely observed life cycles of plants and animals. Through time the Great Round was accepted as a way of looking at human life as well. The seasonal sprouting, growth, harvest, and dormancy of crops, followed by new life in the spring, was seen as a metaphor for the circling progression of youth to maturity, to old age, to death, and to rebirth into a youthful beginning of a new life. Deeply held myths and rituals, such as the Mysteries of Greece and Egypt, arose around these ideas. With the decline of these civilizations, the Great Round was forgotten.

The work of C. G. Jung (1976) resurrected interest in ancient myths as reflections of archaic layers of the psyche of modern people. The mythic pattern of the Great Round once again became of interest as contemporary researchers grasped its usefulness as a subtle and elegant alternative to strictly linear models of human development. Joan Kellogg, an art therapist who worked with Stanislas Grof as part of a research team at the Maryland Psychiatric Research Center during the 1970s, made important discoveries about the relationship of the ancient paradigm of the Great Round to the ever-changing quality of human consciousness. Kellogg (1984, 1982) identified twelve archetypal patterns, or stages, of human functioning that link together in a repeating cycle of growth. The archetypal stages of the Great Round described by Kellogg begin with experiences of confusion, depression, and diffused consciousness, and progress through stages of dawning awareness, the refinement of ego identity, increasing motivation, and organized effort toward a personal goal. With the attainment of a goal the person arrives at stages that bring a decline in functioning and demand the surrender of attachments to what has been in order to enter once again into the stage of dark liminality where the seeds of a new beginning are planted.

After study with Kellogg I found her model of the Great Round useful in my work with clients, and also for understanding my own cycling through life's ups and downs. Naturally I turned to the Great Round to help make sense of my inner journey through menopause. For simplicity I grouped Kellogg's twelve stages into a journey through four levels: The Call, the Below, the Ascent, and the New Order. I created the Litany of the Great Round to celebrate the steps of a journey through change. It is a cycle of prayers and responses based on the twelve archetypal stages of human consciousness identified by Kellogg, arranged to begin where my initiation into crone-dom began, with those stages marked by completion, loss, descent, and a time below in darkness. The prayers continue with

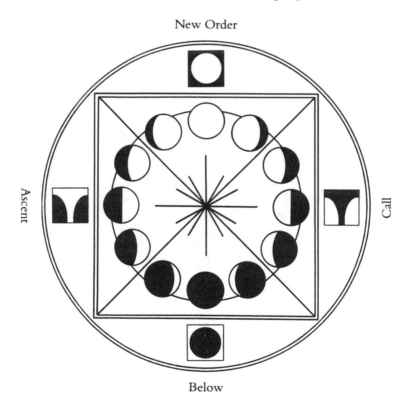

Twelve archetypal stages of change are grouped into the cyclical progression of the Call, the Below, Ascent, and the New Order.

the experience of ascent through stages of rebuilding, and finally accomplishment and completion.

The Litany of the Great Round brings alive in the eternal present of ritual space an experience of personal transformation. Prayers can be excerpted from the litany and made part of personal rituals that meet the needs of the moment. The litany may also be used as the structure for a year-long ritual concentrating on a single prayer each month. Some may wish to transcribe the prayers into a journal or a personal book of prayers as a form of active meditation.

I have used the litany in its entirety for ritual observances of the completion of a cycle. When using it with a group, I like to arrange chairs in a circle and place a prayer under each chair. After ritual space is opened people take turns reading the prayers aloud in order from beginning (Crystallization) to end (Functioning Ego). After each prayer the whole group reads the response together. In this way the group moves through the entire cycle of change metaphorically, honoring each stage along the way.

This is a powerful experience for those in the group. As it often happens, the prayer that chance gives you to read is most fitting and expressive of where you are in your life. Hearing the prayers for those stages opposite where you are in the circle is a reminder of where you have been and will be again. This is an encouraging, humbling, awesome reminder of the ongoing cycle of renewal. Something in the litany will touch each person in the group, resonating with where they are at that moment.

When creating a ritual for a specific time in the Journey, part of the litany can be used along with other actions. For example, a ceremony for Ascent might consist of quiet meditation in the garden gazing on bulbs planted earlier, now sprouted into beautiful flowers. A reading aloud of litany prayers for the Labyrinth, the Beginning, or the Target, followed by the refrain "I accept the gifts that this moment brings," could accompany the task of working special nourishment into the soil around the flowers: tears, water from last night's cooking pot, a few drops of blood.

The litany might also become part of a marriage ceremony that establishes a new order. The pledge of the prayer Squaring the Circle could be spoken before a group of friends and sealed with a kiss, a toast, or the sharing of an apple cut in two. When living through the Below, a silent reading of the prayer for the Void could be followed by quiet reflection on what the schedule of the day holds and how best to allocate your energy to do what must be done. For someone receiving the Call through being unexpectedly laid off at work, writing the prayer for Gates of Death into a personal journal could be followed by letters written there, with no intention of being sent, to those who were the instrument of the change.

In its simplest form, the refrain "I accept the gifts that this moment brings" can be repeated as an affirmation amid the busyness of everyday life. Speaking this phrase also serves as a reminder of the larger pattern of which your life is a part. Seeing the form of the Great Round as it plays out in your life can give you permission to enjoy to the fullest the richness of now, knowing it will not last forever. It can be a comforting reminder that though you are stymied in confusion now, there is no blame, and there will be clarity, energy, and productivity again, when the time is right.

Expanding the Litany of the Great Round into a ritual cycle for the whole year aligns the energies of the prayers with the rhythms of the natural world. Beginning with the Void in the month of January, a different prayer is used for meditation, journaling, and creating rituals each month. I find that working with the imagery of the prayers through the seasons deepens my connection with the rhythms of nature and helps me celebrate my own inner life as part of nature too.

Those who want to live even more deeply into the meaning of the prayers may wish to do as I did: create your own personal prayer book by transcribing the Litany of the Great Round into a blank book. Illustrate the book with your drawings, pictures from magazines, or personal photographs that speak to you of your journey. With friends who have also made prayer books, exciting new possibilities open up for community rituals.

I have shared some suggestions for creating rituals to honor your own journey. Let them be an inspiration for you in thinking of others that uniquely suit you and the reasons you are making a ritual. Create your rituals for the good of yourself and others, with no intentions to injure or do harm. You will find, as I have, that personally created rituals can heal you, support your journey of growth on the Great Round, bring ordinary daily activities alive with fresh meaning, and mark important turning points in your life. The next chapter presents the text of the Litany of the Great Round, given here for your use in creating rituals.

9

Litany of the Great Round

Opening

Creator God, who is above and below, far and near, within and without, be here now with us in this gathering. You who brought into being all creatures, bless us with your presence. For you and you alone make this place sacred, and your fragrance heals us. Your sun, moon, and stars bring us light and teach us the rhythms of the universe. From you, who place around us so abundantly all the wonders of nature, we learn of life, death, and love. Hear our words and be with your people now as we open sacred space and make ceremony for the good of all who share this, our earthen home.

 ## The Call

Crystallization

O God, my creator, I give thanks for the completion of my undertaking. As the rose fulfills itself by blooming, so have I lived out my being in the world by bringing into reality my inspiration. In ways I know and cannot know, the completion of this labor expresses my true purpose. With this moment all my striving to be, to know, to love, and to create resolves into a rich tapestry of wholeness. The harvest is gathered in, and its spiritual food nourishes me. I willingly relinquish my personal claims to what I have accomplished, knowing that it was in your service that my work was done and through your help that the deeds were performed.

REFRAIN: I accept the gifts that this moment brings.

Gates of Death

O God, that which once gave me such pleasure is now empty and without meaning. I am stunned by the end of contentment. Your design is no longer known to me. I am pulled apart as I strain to stay above the dark abyss of the unknown, yet I feel myself sinking into fiery darkness. I place myself in your hands, knowing that you will send me nothing I cannot endure, nothing that will not teach me, and nothing that will not open me yet more to the experience of your love. I pray your blessings on my loved ones who must suffer with me this time of trial. Sustain them when I am not there, give them understanding when I am bewildered, bless them with patience to endure these dark times in our journey together.

REFRAIN: I accept the gifts that this moment brings.

Fragmentation

Lord, I am lost and I do not know how to find myself. You have turned your face away from me, and my cries are mute in my throat. My food has no taste, I cannot see what is before me through my tears, my heart is numb with grief and suffering. This dark night sits like a dangerous beast upon my chest. I am its prisoner. Yet I remember this place within my bones, and they whisper, "Hold on. Hold on." Once again I learn: you do not according to my will, but I according to yours. O God! I accept this suffering, knowing that this dark path, too, is a human life, and trusting that the sadness I hold will create a place where joy can come. Here, as in the light, I sing in awe the perfection of your love.

REFRAIN: I accept the gifts that this moment brings.

 # Below

Transcendent Ecstasy

O God, here I rest, soft and broken, in the belly of the whale, knowing the pearl is nearby but hidden in the dark. You lift me up gently with your wings, sheltering me there in peace so that I can see the path I have traveled: through light and dark, through joy and sorrow, through emptiness and abundance. You show me the circling of my path, and at last I understand the purpose of the suffering, the necessity of the happiness. All is there, nothing is lost, in the weaving of my life. Seeing my place in your creation, I rejoice. My heart bursts open with love. Receiving your grace, I am ablaze with light at the center of darkness.

REFRAIN: I accept the gifts that this moment brings.

Void

Blessed Goddess, I see you not, and yet your heavy weight is upon me. All is darkness. I am lost to myself, utterly lost and alone in this alien place without boundaries. I sleep a deep, dreamless sleep, your hand upon my face. Yet I have fevered remembrances of you. There was once warmth, love, and tenderness. Will there be again? There was once color, dancing, and savory foods to eat. Will there be again? There was once thought, knowing, and decision. Will there be again? Surrendering all hope, I wait like a seed that is buried in the cold earth of winter. Just as it breaks free in the spring, I trust that I too will emerge from this dark place, reborn to serve you as other creatures do, by growing to become that one I am meant to be.

REFRAIN: I accept the gifts that this moment brings.

Bliss

O warm Mother Goddess, I swim in your boundless ocean. Your sweet taste pleasures me. Your fragrant scent teaches me of roses, lilies, and passionflowers. All things are given as I float peacefully in you. Your arms encircle me round and hold me close in this gentle world. Somewhere light sparkling like diamonds fills me with wonder, but my sleepy eyes cannot gaze for long upon the sight. In drowsy forgetfulness I stretch my limbs and feel your body next to mine, soft, strong, and reassuring. It is enough that I am rocked by your gentle movements. In this place we are as one together. Bless me, Mother, for I am your child.

REFRAIN: I accept the gifts that this moment brings.

 # Ascent

Labyrinth

Mother, you have touched me and I am quickened! Your long hair floats in the water, telling me you are near. Stretching tall, I test growing muscle and strengthening bone. Before my eyes a path unfolds, and I am pulled forward on a journey to find you and, in the searching, to discover myself. Twisting, turning, I climb through new worlds, encountering strange creatures, marveling at shape-shifters who swim from fish to bird, to star, then back again to fish. Sometimes the footing is slippery, but I press on. I fly up, I shimmy down, I cling as the path spins round and round, but always I am on the way. And as I travel, I am changing, rearranging, expanding, contracting, pushing and tugging, spiraling in and out. Seeking you, I am pulled forward into life.

REFRAIN: I accept the gifts that this moment brings.

Beginning

Mother, I have found you! Always you were here, but I was too close to see. Your beautiful face shines like the sun. Your smile warms me. Your soft, flowing hair smells of lilacs, chamomile, and honey. I sit upon your lap as on a throne, supported by your strong back and knowing hands. From your own body you feed me all that I need and more. I take courage from your delight in me, and I find myself worthy of being. Rooted in your pleasure, my selfhood grows like a flower planted near gently flowing water. In finding you, I have discovered myself as well. Help me fulfill my destiny to be a person.

REFRAIN: I accept the gifts that this moment brings.

Target

Mother, your arms circling me round once felt so safe and warm. Now I have grown and they are tight and unwelcome like a prison from which I must break free. Give me the strength to put behind me the soft world of a mother's child. I would press forward from being into doing, and yet I am pushed and pulled by indecision. My anger burns hot, and my fear carries me away to cold places. My loved ones are puzzled and withdraw when I say "Hold me close! Let me go!" Mother, help me stir the pot a little longer while it boils. Keep the fire hot. Let me feel the sting of your spattering words and the rising steam of my emotion so that I may stir myself into action. For through these trials I will lay down the boundaries of myself and claim my birthright to be, to know, to love, and to create.

REFRAIN: I accept the gifts that this moment brings.

 ## New Order

Dragon Fight

Goddess, teach me my name! Guide my feet upon the path to the center of the earth, and give me a warrior's courage to face the beast that waits for me there, for I would claim a place for myself in the domain of my ancestors. Help me to challenge the ways of my parents and my parents' parents, that I may take of theirs what is useful to me, release that which is not needed, and forgive that which causes me pain. Reveal to me my own purpose. Touch my hands as I learn new skills, and open my heart for the understanding of new ideas. As I grow in strength and sureness, initiate in me the ability to love myself and another. Teach me what it is to be a woman, what it is to be a man.

REFRAIN: I accept the gifts that this moment brings.

Squaring the Circle

Thanks to you, Mother Goddess, Father God, for revealing this glimpse of the wholeness of all things in perfectly balanced opposites. Male and female, dark and light, good and evil take up their endless dance before my eyes as you bestow upon me the gift of consciousness. Henceforth I wield the sword of discrimination, separating this from that. Yet your sacred union of male and female has within it too the pattern of harmony that smooths the clash of opposites. In the balance of this centerpoint I celebrate myself and rejoice in my loving heart, my pulsing body, and my yearning soul. The quest is begun. The tools of craft are given. Engage my heart, mind, body, and soul in the service of your design for me. Join me to this other, this work, this creation, and draw from deep within me the fearless constancy to see my pledge through to the end.

REFRAIN: I accept the gifts that this moment brings.

Functioning Ego

Father God, I accept the powerful gifts you offer: the ability to know what has not been known, the impulse to create something never seen, the power to lead and shape the world of human beings. As I bring my dreams into reality with the labor of my own hands, the work is hard, but it gives me pleasure. These things I do, not for glory, but in fulfillment of the pattern written within me at my making. I pray you protect me in my strivings from the temptation to swallow your power and deny my fragile human life. May your beauty go before me to guide my feet upon the path with heart. And let me live that I may know in full measure the joy, the pain, and the mystery of the life ways you have given me.

REFRAIN: I accept the gifts that this moment brings.

Closing

Our thanks to you, Creator, for your presence in this gathering. As we have walked the circle of life in sacred space, we have been touched by memories, strengthened with understanding, and quickened with hope. Stay with us now in our hearts as we leave this sacred time and place to pick up the threads of our lives, set aside for this moment with you. For though this ceremony comes to a close, we know that your presence in our lives is without end. We thank you for your blessings on us and all beings with whom we share this ever turning world, and we accept the gifts that this moment brings.

References

Beck, Renée, and Sydney Barbara Metrick. 1990. *The Art of Ritual.* Berkeley, Calif.: Celestial Arts.

Budapest, Zsuzsanna. *Grandmother Moon: Lunar Magic in Our Lives.* San Francisco: Harper San Francisco, 1989.

———. *The Grandmother of Time: A Woman's Book of Celebrations, Spells, and Sacred Objects for Every Month of the Year.* San Francisco: Harper San Francisco, 1989.

———. *The Holy Book of Women's Mysteries.* Wingbow Press, 1989.

Campbell, Joseph. 1971. *The Hero with a Thousand Faces.* New York: World Publishing Co.

Carotenuto, Aldo. 1986. *The Spiral Way: A Woman's Healing Journey.* Tr. John Shepley. Toronto: Inner City Books.

Castillejo, Irene Claremont de. 1973. *Knowing Woman: A Feminine Psychology.* New York: Harper and Row.

Cirlot, J. E. 1962. *A Dictionary of Symbols.* 2d ed. Tr. Jack Sage. New York: Philosophical Library.

Corbett, Lionel. 1988. "Transformation of the Image of God Leading to Self-Initiation into Old Age," pp. 371–88. In *Betwixt and Between: Patterns of Masculine and Feminine Initiation.* Edited by Louise Carus Mahdi, Steven Foster, and Meredith Little. La Salle, Ill.: Open Court.

Douglas, Mary. 1973. *Natural Symbols.* 2d ed. London: Barrie and Jenkins.

Downing, Christine. 1991. *Journey through Menopause: A Personal Rite of Passage.* New York: Crossroads.

Driver, Tom F. 1991. *The Magic of Ritual.* New York: HarperSan-Francisco.

Duerk, Judith. 1989. *Circle of Stones: Woman's Journey to Herself.* San Diego: Lura Media.

Edinger, Edward F. 1987. *Ego and Archetype.* New York: Penguin Books.

Eliade, Mircea. 1991a. *Images and Symbols: Studies in Religious Symbolism.* Princeton: Princeton University Press.

————. 1991b. *The Myth of the Eternal Return, Or Cosmos and History.* Tr. Willard R. Trask. Princeton, N.J.: Princeton University Press.

————. 1994. *Rites and Symbols of Initiation.* 2d ed. Tr. Willard R. Trask. Dallas: Spring Publications.

Fincher, Susanne F. 1991. *Creating Mandalas: For Insight, Healing, and Self-Expression.* Boston and London: Shambhala Publications.

Frazer, James George. 1950. *The Golden Bough.* New York: Macmillan.

Graves, Robert. 1960. *The Greek Myths.* Vols. 1 and 2. New York: Penguin Books.

Harding, M. Esther. 1976. *Woman's Mysteries Ancient and Modern.* New York: Harper and Row.

Johnson, Robert A. 1986. *Inner Work: Using Dreams and Active Imagination for Personal Growth.* San Francisco: Harper and Row.

Jung, C. G. 1959. *Aion: Researches into the Phenomenology of the Self.* 2d ed. Tr. R.F.C. Hull. Princeton, N.J.: Princeton University Press.

————. 1973. *C. G. Jung: Letters.* Vol. 1: 1906–1950. Selected and edited by Gerhard Adler and Aniela Jaffé. Princeton, N.J.: Princeton University Press.

————. 1976. *Symbols of Transformation,* 2nd ed. Tr. R.F.C. Hull. Princeton, N.J.: Princeton University Press.

————. 1990. *The Archetypes and the Collective Unconscious.* 2d ed. Tr. R.F.C. Hull. Princeton, N.J.: Princeton University Press.

Kaberry, Phyllis M. 1939. *Aboriginal Woman: Sacred and Profane.* New York: Humanities Press.

Kellogg, Joan. 1984. "Mandala: Path of Beauty." Master's thesis, Antioch University, Columbia, Md.

Kellogg, Joan, and F. B. DiLeo. 1982. "Archetypal Stages of the Great Round of Mandala." *Journal of Religion and Psychical Research* 5:38–49.

Kerényi, Karoly. 1967. *Eleusis: Archetypal Image of Mother and Daughter.* Tr. Ralph Manheim. New York: Bollingen Foundation.

Langer, Susanne K. 1976. *Philosophy in a New Key: A Study in the Symbolism of Reason, Rite, and Art.* 3d ed. Cambridge: Harvard University Press.

Lex, Barbara W. 1979. "The Neurobiology of Ritual Trance," pp. 117–51. In *The Spectrum of Ritual: A Biogenetic Structural Analysis.* Edited by Eugene G. d'Aquili, Charles D. Laughlin, Jr., and John McManus. New York: Columbia University Press.

Lincoln, Bruce. 1981. *Emerging from the Chrysalis: Studies in Rituals of Women's Initiation.* Cambridge and London: Harvard University Press.

Mankowitz, Ann. 1984. *Change of Life: A Psychological Study of Dreams and the Menopause.* Toronto: Inner City Books.

Mead, Margaret. 1928. *Coming of Age in Samoa.* New York: William Morrow and Co.

Meehan, Aidan. 1991. *Celtic Design: Knotwork, the Secret Method of the Scribes.* New York: Thames and Hudson.

Mindell, Arnold. 1982. *Dreambody: The Body's Role in Revealing the Self.* Boston: Sigo Press.

Murdock, Maureen. *The Heroine's Journey.* Boston: Shambhala Publications, 1990.

Nelson, Gertrud M. 1986. *To Dance with God.* New York: Paulist Press.

Perera, Sylvia Brinton. 1981. *Descent to the Goddess: A Way of Initiation for Women.* Toronto: Inner City Books.

Pretat, Jane R. 1994. *Coming to Age: The Croning Years and Late-Life Transformation.* Toronto: Inner City Books.

Ross, Mary Lou Skinner. 1981. *Thoughts While Ironing.* Privately published.

Saint John of the Cross. 1959. *Dark Night of the Soul.* 3d ed. Tr. E.

Allison Peers. Garden City, N.Y.: Image Books, Doubleday and Co.

Shorter, Bani. 1988. *An Image Darkly Forming: Women and Initiation.* London: Routledge.

Starhawk. *Truth or Dare.* San Francisco: Harper San Francisco, 1989.

Stein, Murray. 1994. *In Midlife: A Jungian Perspective.* Dallas, Texas: Spring Publications.

Stein, Jan O., and Murray Stein, 1988. Psychotherapy, initiation, and the midlife transition, pp. 287–303. In *Betwixt and Between: Patterns of Masculine and Feminine Initiation.* Edited by Louise Carus Mahdi, Steven Foster and Meredith Little. La Salle, Ill.: Open Court.

Stevens, Anthony. 1982. *Archetypes: A Natural History of the Self.* New York: William Morrow and Co.

Stone, Merlin. *When God Was a Woman.* New York: Harcourt Brace, 1978.

Taylor, Dena, and Amber Coverdale Sumrall, eds. 1991. *Women of the 14th Moon: Writing on Menopause.* Freedom, Calif.: Crossing Press.

Taylor, Sofia Fillmore. 1992. "A Croning Ceremony." *Crone Chronicles,* Fall Equinox: 33.

Turner, Victor. 1967. *The Forest of Symbols: Aspects of Ndembu Ritual.* Ithaca and London: Cornell University Press.

———. 1969. *The Ritual Process: Structure and Anti-Structure.* Chicago: Aldine.

———. 1988. Betwixt and Between: The liminal period in rites of passage, pp. 3–22. In *Betwixt and Between: Patterns of Masculine and Feminine Initiation.* Edited by Louise Carus Mahdi, Steven Foster and Meredith Little. La Salle, Ill.: Open Court.

Ulanov, Ann Belford. 1971. *The Feminine.* Evanston: Northwestern University Press.

Van der Hart, Onno. 1983. *Rituals in Psychotherapy: Transitions and Continuity.* Tr. Angie Pleit-Kuiper. New York: Irvington Publishers.

Van Gennep, Arnold. 1960. *The Rites of Passage.* Chicago: University of Chicago Press.

Walker, Barbara G. 1985. *The Crone: Woman of Age, Wisdom, and Power.* San Francisco: Harper and Row.

———. 1988. *The Woman's Dictionary of Symbols and Sacred Objects.* San Francisco: Harper and Row.

———. 1990. *Women's Rituals: A Sourcebook.* New York: Harper-SanFrancisco.

Weed, Susun S. 1992. *Menopausal Years the Wise Woman Way: Alternative Approaches for Women 30–90.* Woodstock, N.Y.: Ash Tree Publishing.

Wilhelm, Richard 1981. *The I Ching or Book of Changes.* 3d ed. Tr. Cary F. Baynes. Princeton, N.J.: Princeton University Press.

Wing, R. L. 1982. *Illustrated I Ching.* Garden City, N.Y.: Dolphin Books, Doubleday and Co.

Wisechild, Louise M. 1988. *The Obsidian Mirror.* Seattle, Wash.: Seal Press.

Woodman, Marion. 1985. *The Pregnant Virgin.* Toronto: Inner City Books.

Young-Eisendrath, Polly, and Florence Wiedemann. 1987. *Female Authority.* New York: Guilford.